CHAUTAUQUA SERENADE

Caitlin Press Inc.
8100 Alderwood Road
Halfmoon Bay, BC V0N 1Y1
www.caitlin-press.com

Text design by Benjamin Dunfield and Vici Johnstone
Cover design by Vici Johnstone
Copy edit by Kathleen Fraser

All visual material comes from the Ruth Bowers family collection unless otherwise stated. Items from the Redpath Chautauqua collection at the Special Collections Library of the University of Iowa are labeled Redpath Chautauqua Collection, UI, and used by permission.

Printed in Canada

Caitlin Press Inc. acknowledges financial support from the Government of Canada and the Canada Council for the Arts, and from the Province of British Columbia through the British Columbia Arts Council and the Book Publisher's Tax Credit.

Canada Council   Conseil des Arts   BRITISH COLUMBIA   Canada   Canada
for the Arts   du Canada   ARTS COUNCIL

Library and Archives Canada Cataloguing in Publication

Sherwood, Jay, 1947-, author
    Chautauqua serenade : violinist Ruth Bowers on tour, 1910-1912 / Jay Sherwood.

ISBN 978-1-927575-69-7 (paperback)

    1. Bowers, Ruth, 1888-1982. 2. Violinists—United States—Biography.
3. Chautauquas. I. Title.

ML418.B786S55 2015   787.2092   C2015-904041-8

CHAUTAUQUA SERENADE

Violinist Ruth Bowers on Tour
1910–1912

Jay Sherwood

Caitlin Press

Dedicated to Ruth Bowers and all the people who made her chautauqua and lyceum tours such a memorable time in her life.

Meet me
at Chautauqua
"Joy Night"

CONTENT

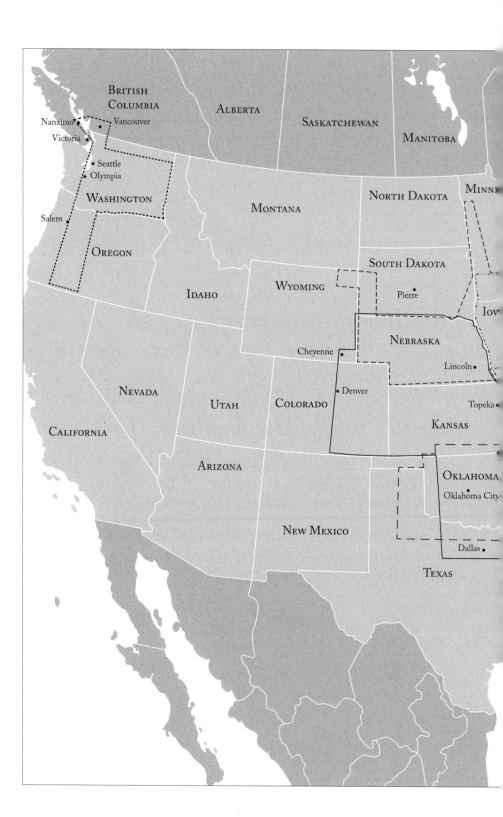

The Tours of Ruth Bowers, 1910-1912

- - - - - - January–March 1910 Lyceum Tour – Ramos' Spanish Orchestra
.... May–October 1910 Chautauqua Tour – Elma B. Smith Company
- — — - November–December 1910 Lyceum tour – Elma B. Smith Company
.... January–March 1911 Lyceum Tour – Elma B. Smith Company
-..—..-.. June–September 1911 Chautauqua Tour – Clarke-Bowers Company
———— June–August 1912 Chautauqua tour – Ruth Bowers Company

Forest City

July 17 to July 23

O. E. BEHYMER
Superintendent

GEO. B. MANGOLD
Morning Hour Lecturer

PROGRAMS BEGIN PROMPTLY

Scouts ....9:00 a. m.   Morning Lecture 10:00
Afternoon Music ....2:30   Afternoon Lecture 3:00
Evening Music ....7:30   Evening Lecture 8:15

MONDAY

AFTERNOON—Opening Exercises and Important Announcements
Music by DUNBAR SINGING ORCHESTRA
Popular Lecture
"The Other Fellow"   DR. WALTER MANSELL
EVENING—Concert by   DUNBAR SINGING ORCHESTRA
Humorous Lecture
"The Mission of Mirth"   THOMAS McCLARY

TUESDAY

"Scout Camps" for the Children
Morning Lecture—"The Emancipation of Woman"
AFTERNOON—Music by   WEATHERWAX BROS. QUARTET
Popular Lecture
"Old Days in Dixie"   MISS BELLE KEARNEY
EVENING—Concert by   WEATHERWAX BROS. QUARTET
Monologue
"The Sign of the Cross"   JAMES FRANCIS O'DONNELL

WEDNESDAY

"Scout Camps" for the Children
Morning Lecture—"The Social Discontent"
AFTERNOON—Music by   CLARKE-BOWERS COMPANY
Lecture by   HON. W. J. BRYAN
EVENING—Concert by   CLARKE-BOWERS COMPANY
Lecture (Illustrated) Beautiful Slides and Motion Pictures
"Storm Heroes of Our Coasts"   HON. ARTHUR K. PECK

THURSDAY

"Scout Camps" for the Children
Morning Lecture—"The Children of the Poor"
AFTERNOON—Music by   THE WHITE ROSE ORCHESTRA
Travel Lecture
"A Giant in Pigmy Land"   DR. WILLIAM EDGAR GEIL
EVENING—Concert by   THE WHITE ROSE ORCHESTRA
Lecture
"The Era of Conscience"   HON. JOSEPH W. FOLK

PRELUDE

Forest City, Iowa—July 19, 1911

It's chautauqua week in Forest City, the town's biggest event of the year. There will be over thirty programs from a variety of traveling performers who will provide education and entertainment. Thaviu's International Band will play; Garetta and his trained animals and birds will entertain; the popular Weatherwax Brothers Quartet will sing; there will be lectures; and several other musical groups will play. The big chautauqua tent has been put up and the town is alive with activity.

Today is a special day. Over six thousand people have been on the chautauqua grounds and about 1,600, more than the entire population of the town, have filled the chautauqua tent early to hear a lecture by William Jennings Bryan, a three-time candidate for the United States presidency and a man many people believe to be the finest American orator of the early twentieth century. Bryan is only speaking at a few locations in Iowa this summer, so that makes his appearance at Forest City even more important. His booming, resonant voice will fill the chautauqua tent and carry out onto the surrounding grounds.

But before Bryan delivers his lecture, the program will begin, like most afternoon chautauqua sessions, with a half-hour musical concert. Today the performance will be by the Clarke-Bowers Company. The pianist is Grace Desmond, a young lady from Chicago who is on her first chautauqua tour. Grace will be the accompanist and play a solo. C. Edward Clarke, "the Canadian baritone," will sing. He has played on the chautauqua and lyceum circuits and is considered one of their rising stars. Clarke's rich clear voice will carry throughout the chautauqua tent. The violinist is Ruth Bowers, a young woman from Erie, Pennsylvania. During the past eighteen months she has been on tour from coast to coast and from Texas to Canada. Her music will include the sweet sounds of a serenade.

When they perform, can you hear them?

OPPOSITE PAGE: A schedule for the chautauqua programs in Forest City.

Ruth and a friend relaxing between performances on the 1911 chautauqua circuit.

PREFACE

I have many fond memories of my grandmother, Ruth Bowers, for when I was young, she regularly spent the weekend at our house. She was always interested in what I was doing and I spent a lot of time talking with her. I knew that music was an important part of her life: she played the violin, and when she was young she had traveled around the United States, performing on chautauqua tours.

When I was seven, my great-grandmother died and Ruth moved back to Erie, Pennsylvania (where she was born and raised), to care for her elderly father. The following summer I went by myself to Erie for a week. It was my first time away from home, as well as my first airplane ride. With two stewardesses and four passengers on the flight from Pittsburgh to Buffalo to Erie, I was treated royally. One evening I went with my great-grandfather and four of his friends to my first chautauqua concert. At eighty-nine my great-grandfather was the oldest person in the group, while the driver, at seventy-nine, was the youngest. During the hour-long drive to Chautauqua, New York, we passed through a few small towns and invariably the community's cemetery. This would prompt one of the men to comment that it wouldn't be long before they would be in a similar place, and jocular remarks by others in the group would follow. At Chautauqua we walked through the historic town and attended a musical program at the amphitheater. It was a special evening.

My great-grandfather died the following year. Ruth decided to remain in Erie and live at the family home and the week-long trip to Erie became an annual occasion for me. Since the house where my grandmother lived was close to both the waterfront and downtown, there were lots of places to visit.

During that week I would spend part of an afternoon in the attic. This was accessed through a small room that had been my great-grandmother's studio for painting and sewing. Climbing a small stepladder, pushing open a half-sizes door, I would boost myself onto a small landing and walk up a few steps to the main part of the attic. One side had a floor and window, and here much of the family history was kept. Some of my great-grandmother's paintings resided there, turned against the wall. One trunk contained items from my great-great-grandfather, D.P. Robbins, including his Civil War diary and the health pamphlets that he wrote. In the bottom of another trunk were the postcards and letters from my grandmother's chautauqua and lyceum tours. I loved to look at the pictures, read the cards and letters, and try to imagine what it was like to tour the United States years ago. Downstairs Ruth had a photo album of her 1911 and 1912 chautauqua tours. Occasionally she would bring it out and talk about her experiences. The pictures of the crew boys always brought a smile to her lips and a twinkle to her eyes. It had been a joyous time for her—the wonderful people that she met and the friendships she made; the opportunity to travel; and above all else, the chance to play her violin to audiences that were eager to hear live musical programs.

For my mother's ninetieth birthday, I wanted to produce a booklet about my grandmother's time on tour. My cousins Karen and Terri lent me the material that they held, and their assistance was invaluable. Along with the items that I had, I began assembling the specifics of the six chautauqua and lyceum tours that Ruth made from 1910 to 1912. My grandmother's material was supplemented by three research trips to the University of Iowa Special Collections and their large chautauqua fonds. Here I found more material about Ruth and some of the people that she performed with. I would like to express my thanks to Kathy Hodson for her expert assistance during my time there in the spring of 2013 and two subsequent research trips. Kathy, who has been a mentor for many chautauqua researchers, willingly shared her knowledge of circuit chautauqua and the extensive collection that is housed at the University of Iowa.

Jane Westenfield at the Allegheny College library in Meadville, Pennsylvania, helped me during my research of the chautauqua material in their collection. Carol Kirsch from the Iowa State Historical Society and Jan Perone from the Abraham Lincoln Presidential Library in Springfield, Illinois, located additional newspaper articles that provided more information about my grandmother's performances and what the chautauqua and lyceum programs were like. My thanks also go to the people in several small communities who sent newspaper accounts of my grandmother's performances in their towns, and to the staff at the Kansas Historical Society who assisted me during my research of their newspaper collection.

I was also fortunate to make contact with Pat Biallas, who has a family history website. Her aunt, Grace Desmond, was on a chautauqua tour with Ruth in 1911. Through Pat I was able to fill in many details about the friendship that Ruth and Grace established that summer, providing a better and more meaningful understanding of this tour.

As I learned more about Ruth's adventures and read the chautauqua literature, I began to realize that my grandmother's unpublished material provided relevant information about the early years of circuit chautauqua. I also recognized that the newspaper articles about the chautauqua and lyceum programs were a rich and largely underutilized source of information that provided a better understanding of the journalism of small-town newspapers of the time. To portray the material as accurately as possible, I have retained the original punctuation and formatting used in quotes from primary sources like letters and newspapers.

What started as a family history project has evolved into *Chautauqua Serenade,* an account of the experiences of a performer on the chautauqua and lyceum circuits over a century ago. I would like to thank Vici Johnstone of Caitlin Press for publishing this book as part of her ongoing mandate to support publications about adventurous women.

Most performers had their own publicity brochure. This is the cover of Ruth's brochure when she played on the 1911 Redpath-Vawter Chautauqua circuit.

INTRODUCTION

In the early twentieth century, the chautauqua summer circuits and the lyceum programs held during the fall and winter were the main form of live entertainment for much of rural North America. Chautauqua lecturers and musicians gave programs to millions of Americans and Canadians. A large number of the lecturers were household names at that time, and many of the musicians were well-known professional performers. In the fall and winter some communities arranged a series of programs through lyceum bureaus. Several of the lecturers and musicians who were on the summer chautauqua tours also played on the lyceum circuit. Although the chautauqua circuits only lasted about twenty-five years, they had an important impact on American culture during the early twentieth century. President Theodore Roosevelt was quoted as saying that chautauqua is "the most American thing in America."

From 1910 to 1912, my grandmother, Ruth Bowers, was on tour as a violinist performing on three chautauqua circuits and three lyceum tours. She played at towns from the Atlantic seaboard to the Pacific coast, and from Texas to British Columbia, but most of her programs were in the Midwest.

Ruth frequently sent postcards to her parents, her boyfriend, Charles Gibson (Gibby), and her brother, Everett. She also wrote letters. Most of the ones sent to her mother and some of the letters to Gibby still exist. They provide details of performances, daily life offstage and travel. Ruth frequently described the hospitality shown by people in the towns where she played and the special activities she took part in. She collected memorabilia and had a scrapbook of newspaper clippings from many of the towns where she played. Ruth made notes about most of the locations where she performed on the 1911 chautauqua circuit. And during the summers of 1911 and 1912, she took a camera, photographing events on the chautauqua circuit, several well-known chautauqua performers offstage and some of the communities where she played.

A large portion of the material from her years on tour has survived, and almost all of it is previously unpublished. In *The Romance of Small-Town Chautauquas*, James Schultz writes about the experiences of his father and uncle, who were supervisors on the chautauqua circuits during the height of the movement, and he includes material that they collected.

In *Chautauqua Serenade* I have used my grandmother's writing, photographs and mementos to provide insight into chautauqua and lyceum tours during the early years of the movement. This has been supplemented by articles, for newspapers in almost all of the towns where chautauqua and lyceum programs were held reported on the event, and they usually provided some coverage of Ruth's performance. These articles also illustrate the style and language used in rural community newspapers.

Ruth's experiences were typical of most performers on the chautauqua and lyceum circuits at that time. However, few performers, even the ones who were household names in the early twentieth century, have detailed records of their daily life and experiences while they were on tour. Ruth's written accounts and the newspaper articles about her programs show that she strove to achieve a high level of performance, both in her violin playing and in her selection of music. But the performances, practice and travel were only part of the activities. On most days there were a few hours of free time. This sometimes included automobile rides across the countryside, boat trips, stagecoach rides or walks. Occasionally there were special activities in the towns where they were staying. The chautauqua and lyceum tours provided people like Ruth with an opportunity to have fun and a freedom that was very rare for women during that era. The pictures that Ruth took in 1911 and 1912 express the joy of being on tour.

In the early twentieth century, there were three main occupations for women who wanted to work outside the home: teacher, nurse or secretary. For women who were talented and determined there was also the possibility of a career as a musician, whether in chautauqua, vaudeville, symphony or other types of shows. The traveling musicians had an adventurous life available to few women at that time. On tour these women had an opportunity to continue developing their talent by playing to large, enthusiastic audiences and interacting with other musicians. They were independent both financially and in their ability to travel and were recognized for their ability. They stayed in hotels, wore fashionable clothes, met a variety of people and were occasionally entertained at residents' homes in some of the communities. These women musicians were accorded a status that few women achieved at that time. Through the example of their lives they were part of the first wave of the women's liberation movement in the early twentieth century.

By focusing on the experiences of an individual performer, *Chautauqua Serenade* provides an intimate, detailed perspective of life on the early chautauqua circuits and lyceum tours, and it shows what it was like to travel through rural United States in the early twentieth century during all seasons of the year.

THE CHAUTAUQUA AND LYCEUM CIRCUIT

The chautauqua circuit programs of the early twentieth century had their roots in nineteenth-century American culture. In the mid-nineteenth century, literary societies and self-help groups in New England developed community lyceum* programs, bringing professional speakers to their towns to discuss literary and social topics. By the Civil War, the lyceum programs had expanded to much of the eastern United States and into parts of the Midwest. In 1868, James Redpath pioneered the commercial lyceum movement by founding the Redpath Lyceum Bureau in Boston. Three years later he established a regional office in Chicago because of the lyceum's popularity in the Midwest. He booked statesmen, theologians, authors and other prominent people to go on tour and deliver lectures.

The flag is flying and an afternoon performance is in progress at the chautauqua tent.

---

* The word lyceum refers to the garden of the temple of Apollo Lyceus, where the famous Greek philosopher Aristotle lectured his students. A lyceum is an organization sponsoring public programs or a place where such programs are held.

By booking and managing their schedules for a nominal fee, Redpath made it easier for these people to tour the country. Redpath was able to attract many prominent Americans for his tours, and the large audiences who attended the lyceum programs made the movement successful. Redpath sold his lyceum bureau in 1875 but the new owners retained the organization's name and continued to operate and expand it. Although Redpath remained the largest lyceum bureau, others were founded in the late nineteenth century.

Another prominent cultural development was the establishment of the Chautauqua Institution at Lake Chautauqua, New York, in 1874. Initially started as a summer school for Methodist Sunday school teachers, it evolved into an intellectual community with summer-long programs covering a variety of topics and including musical performances. The purpose of the chautauqua programs was to provide both education and entertainment. During the first years, many of the speakers and performers came from New York or New England.

The success of the New York chautauqua prompted many communities in the Midwest to sponsor their own chautauqua programs, which combined local talent and lyceum programs. By the late nineteenth century many lyceum bureaus also operated their own chautauqua circuit.

In 1903, Keith Vawter, an agent for the Redpath Lyceum Bureau, along with his partner, Roy Ellison, established the Standard Redpath Chautauqua under agreement with the parent company. Vawter and Ellison tried to convince the managers of several independent chautauquas in Iowa to let the Standard Redpath Chautauqua provide the program for their communities. Most communities did not want to give up control over their program and Vawter was only able to sign up nine for the 1904 season. To secure more bookings, Ellison and Vawter decided to offer nearby towns that did not have a chautauqua program an opportunity to book with them. They convinced six to join, giving them a total of fifteen venues for this season. All of the new communities needed a facility to hold their program, so Vawter decided to use a circus tent. The tent soon became the visible symbol of the circuit chautauqua.

The 1904 Standard Redpath Chautauqua was not a financial success but it laid the foundation for large-scale circuit chautauqua, which combined the structure of the lyceum program with the chautauqua ideology. The advantage of Vawter's model was that he could establish a uniform program for all of the towns on his circuit. If he could book a sufficient number of communities, he could attract top-caliber talent. Since Vawter arranged all of the details and logistics, the community would only have to provide the financial guarantee and the location.

"How do you like our crew?" The crew boys are setting up a chautauqua tent.

In 1907, Vawter and Ellison, based out of Cedar Rapids, Iowa, operated a Redpath Chautauqua program that traveled to thirty-three towns in Iowa, Nebraska and Wisconsin. The Redpath Chautauqua included more towns the following year and began to achieve financial success. Others followed Vawter's model. In 1906, Alonzo Wilson started the Lincoln Temperance Chautauqua, with its headquarters in Chicago and its main base of operation in Illinois.

After 1907, Vawter's circuit chautauqua expanded and he refined and standardized his program. Vawter developed a seven-day program that he used for almost every town. The chautauqua was held in a tent on a large, open site in the community. Vawter had custom-made brown tents for his chautauqua circuit. Initially the tents could hold about a thousand people, but later, tents were enlarged to accommodate about 1,500 people. The tent had open flaps around the sides in an effort to keep it cool in the summer heat. The flaps could be put down if it got cool or there was inclement weather. The general seats were lumber benches, while the reserved seats were folding chairs. Many people brought cushions to be more comfortable. The tent had lighting, using electricity wherever possible, and there was a sounding board at the back of the stage. Behind the main tent there was a small tent where the performers could change and prepare for their event, and one where the crew boys lived.

During chautauqua week, the community had activities every day. There was a morning session for children. In the midafternoon a musical program, about thirty minutes in length, was followed by a lecture

Gathering for a chautauqua performance. Redpath Chautauqua Collection, University of Iowa.

of about an hour. In the evening, the same musical group performed for forty-five minutes and a different lecturer or entertainer gave a program for at least an hour.

On a weekly chautauqua circuit there would be seven towns holding programs at the same time. While the chautauqua program remained in a town for seven days, the performers moved daily. The musical groups almost always performed in the same order on the seven day circuit. If a musician performed on the second day of the chautauqua in one town, they would travel to the next town that was on its second day of the program and perform there. There was some variation among the lecturers. Occasionally, special orators, like the famous William Jennings Bryan, were only available for certain dates, so the lecturing schedule had to accommodate them.

When a community completed its last chautauqua performance, the tent would be taken down and transported to the next community that was getting ready to start its chautauqua program. Since it took a day to transport and set up the tent, Vawter had eight tents in circulation, even though only seven towns had a chautauqua program operating at a time.

The logistics involved in moving people and equipment were complex. In the early years of circuit chautauqua, travel was almost exclusively by train. Virtually every community in the Midwest had a railroad connection, even if it was only a spur line. There was normally train service at least once a day, bringing passengers, mail and freight to a community. The towns on the chautauqua circuit had to be organized so that travel time and distance were kept to a minimum. Usually the performers played every day, but there were occasional days off, particularly if there was a considerable amount of traveling to a community. The Redpath Chautauqua had to ensure that all of its personnel knew when and where they were traveling on every day of their schedule.

The Redpath-Vawter Chautauqua organization required a large number of people. Behind the scenes there were employees who handled the financial arrangements, booking agents who secured the contract with a town, and advance men and women who handled the advertising, and came to the communities to ensure all the necessary arrangements were made. In town there were the performers, called the talent; the women who ran the morning program for the children and were known as the morning supervisors or junior girls; crew boys who put up and took down the tent; crew who sold the tickets and provided other assistance to make sure that the program went smoothly; and supervisors who were responsible for the overall operation of the chautauqua program in a town.

Women represented a large portion of the audience, for culture was considered important to both women and men, and the circuit chautauquas employed a large number of women for many aspects of their operation. Charlotte Canning writes, "Chautauqua gave young women opportunities they never enjoyed before. Not only was the platform open for dramatic readers, singers and artists of all kinds, but female lecturers were permitted—even encouraged—to troupe the country in greater numbers than the country had seen before." Not only did women perform, but many ran the children's program, acted as supervisors and were involved in the business aspect of the corporations. In "Women in Chautauqua," Austie Wurster notes that women played a greater part in the chautauqua and lyceum circuits than in any other similar organization of that era, and these organizations provided an opportunity for women to show their talent.

Forest City, Iowa, held their fourth annual Redpath-Vawter Chautauqua in 1911. After the event, the *Forest City Summit* wrote: "The Chautauqua for smaller towns, and especially Forest City, is no longer an experiment. Mr. Vawter has established a system especially adapted to cities the size of Forest City and each succeeding year the programs are better and the citizens take not only great interest but pride in making the season a successful one in every sense of the word." The *Summit* also noted that already "fifty of our progressive business men and wide awake farmers have responded to the call for guarantors and signed as a

Lawton High School, Lawton, Okla.

About a thousand people attended the lyceum program in this building in November 1910 when the Elma B. Smith Company (including Ruth Bowers) performed in Lawton.

guarantee for 1912."[1] (Note: Newspaper citations are listed in the Sources Consulted section.)

A town that held a chautauqua program was considered prosperous and progressive in its outlook and could use the event to promote itself to newcomers. To book a chautauqua program, a community would form a committee, usually consisting of prominent local people. The committee would communicate with the Redpath Chautauqua and provide a financial guarantee that they would pay for a certain number of week-long program tickets. Once the contract and date were set, it would be the local committee's responsibility to sell these tickets. If the community had difficulty selling its tickets, the chautauqua would send an agent to assist with sales. Working together to achieve a successful chautauqua program generated civic pride in many small communities. The *Daily News* in Wellington, Kansas, described the process when the final tickets were sold on the opening day of the city's 1912 chautauqua week:

> Last summer fifty business men of Wellington, who believed the Chautauqua to be a good thing, signed a guarantee to the Chautauqua people that the season ticket sales would reach 700. It is the only way the entertainment could be brought back. There was a chance for a small loss to each guarantor, but most of them signed without hesitation, and today the last of the tickets were sold and the guarantee is made good.[2]

After the circuit chautauquas became established and popular, many communities that had a successful chautauqua program would sign up for the following year at the conclusion of their week.

The chautauqua circuits usually lasted for two to three months during the summer, but many larger communities wanted educational programs throughout the fall and winter. The lyceum programs continued to fill that need. A community organization would contract with the lyceum bureau that covered the region for a series of programs, usually five to six, with performances approximately once a month. In October 1909, the *News Journal* in Newcastle, Wyoming, wrote: "In order to get a better class of entertainers than Newcastle has been getting in the past a few of our citizens have arranged with the Redpath-Slayton [lyceum] bureau for five of their best attractions to appear in this city at intervals during the coming season."[3] The bureau would hire performers to travel a circuit, giving a program in several towns. There was normally only one performer at a time in a community, so the performer or company had to be versatile and talented enough to sustain a longer program than one on the chautauqua circuit. This was easy for lecturers but more difficult for musicians and entertainers. Many of the people in the lyceum programs also performed on the chautauqua circuits in the summer. The fall season generally lasted from mid-October until just before Christmas. The winter season began in early January and usually continued until late March. Since fewer communities had lyceum programs, there was more travel involved. Snowstorms occasionally delayed the trains. Cold and inclement weather sometimes limited free-time activities.

The performances normally took place in the town's largest venue. This was often a school gymnasium. Many communities had opera houses that could seat a large number of people. The lyceum programs did not have the visible profile of the chautauqua circuits, but they played an important role in providing culture to many small towns in rural United States.

The local newspaper usually supported a town's chautauqua, because it would receive advertising for the program, and its coverage of the event both before and afterwards would provide plenty of material. Publishers of small-town newspapers had an opportunity to produce journalism that was creative in language and style. Some newspapers provided detailed coverage of the circuit chautauqua that gave readers specific details about the performers and their individual programs. Occasionally, journalists would express an opinion on the importance of the chautauqua or lyceum circuit to the town, and sometimes they would try to describe the personal effects of attending a program. Through reading coverage of the chautauqua circuit (and to a lesser extent the lyceum programs), one can gain a better understanding of the journalism of small-town newspapers in the early twentieth century.

But the most important benefit of chautauqua was to the residents of a town. John Tapia writes in *Circuit Chautauqua*: "The circuit chautauqua programs exposed countless Americans to many new ideas and customs, national and international issues, and popular forms of entertainment that otherwise would have been inaccessible to them. The period of five, six, or seven days set aside for the program also provided opportunities for families, friends and neighbors to visit one another." In 1955, the *Forest City Summit* published an article looking back at the twenty consecutive years that the town had had a chautauqua program. One of the town's committee members recalled that the program was usually in mid-July, when "corn was laid by and farmers could come to town. Visits for relatives and friends were arranged to take advantage of Forest City's time of festival, of reunion, of the special opportunity to hear great speakers, the best in music and entertainment of a light humor. Some annually reserved rooms at the Summit Hotel during the week of Chautauqua."

"A Redpath-Vawter Chautauqua Crowd Homeward Bound." The audience is departing from an afternoon chautauqua program. Redpath Chautauqua Collection, University of Iowa.

The purpose of the chautauqua program was to provide education, entertainment and inspiration to people in small communities. During chautauqua week there would be around thirty programs, about half of them musical, covering a variety of topics and ranging from humorous to serious, from those that had a large educational component to those that were primarily for entertainment. Nationally known people would bring their ideas to rural communities, and professional musicians would provide quality musical programs. With the wide variety of performances, almost everyone could find at least one program they wanted to attend. The *Le Mars Semi-Weekly Sentinel* extolled the benefits of attending the chautauqua program: "At no other place can you get so much of high class entertainment at so low a cost as the Chautauqua. Make next week or part of it a holiday and attend as many sessions as possible. You will be refreshed in body and mind. Hear thirty five first class programs at a cost of less than five cents each."[4] In summarizing the chautauqua program in Hampton, Iowa, the *Franklin County Recorder* wrote: "Every session found the large tent packed with people who came to listen and learn. The programs included some of the best lecturers in the country and some of the finest musical organizations...Each session contained something that contributed in no uncertain way towards better things and higher ideals."[5]

Chautauqua week soon became an important annual event in many towns, generating civic pride. The town would be spruced up and decorated with pennants, banners, window displays and placards. Often there was a parade at the beginning of the week. Some communities set up a campground so that people from the surrounding area could spend the week there. In the early years, the chautauqua circuit companies produced a large folded pamphlet. Inside were descriptions of the performers that week, a schedule and other information. When unfolded, the back side of the pamphlet became a large poster with pictures of the talent who appeared in the community. The pamphlet became a souvenir of chautauqua week and would be a reminder of the event. The 1911 Redpath-Vawter program even included a page on chautauqua etiquette, called "If."

The lecturers, particularly famous people like William Jennings Bryan, were the stars of the circuits, but music was also an important part of the chautauqua program. On most circuits a performance included both a musical program and a lecture, although the lecture was scheduled for a longer time. Since the same musical group usually performed in both the afternoon and the evening, there would be seven different musical groups in a weekly chautauqua. It was important for the managers to choose a wide variety of music for their circuit. This would include vocal and instrumental groups and music that ranged from popular to classical.

"IF"

If you have any criticism to make, make it to the Superintendent. He's paid to listen.

If you have words of praise, tell them to everybody, especially to the out-of-town folks.

If you think the seat you are sitting on is a little hard, remember that soft pine is very scarce in these days of the lumber trust.

If you come late and the program started on time don't complain because you missed something good.

If the musicians on the platform are making so much noise you can scarcely make the person next you hear what you are talking about, just wait till the program is over. Other folks around you would be pleased if you would.

If you have one or two children, don't you think you could take better care of them than to require the platform manager to look after them?

If you like the musicians, encore them. You'll get more for your money if you do and they'll come nearer earning their salary.

If you can possibly do so, attend the morning lectures. It will pay you.

If you have a dog, leave it to watch the premises while you go to Chautauqua. We have tickets for adults and children, but none for dogs.

If you would like to bring your lunch and not go home between the afternoon and evening programs, do so. The tent boys are at your service, even to the sharing of your lunches.

If the platform manager has troubles, offer to help him. He's human and would appreciate it.

If the Chautauqua salute is called for, don't fail to use your handkerchief because it is soiled. Honest dirt is no disgrace.

If it rains and you get a little damp, don't fuss. The crops need the rain.

If somebody advertised to speak fails to appear, remember the fellow that takes his place has a hard job on his hands and needs your help to "make good."

"If," from the 1911 Redpath-Vawter Chautauqua program Redpath Chautauqua Collection, University of Iowa.

Our trunks have arrived. C. Edward Clarke, front; Ruth Bowers, middle left; and Grace Desmond of the Clarke-Bowers Company on a baggage car at a train station in Iowa in 1911. Lecturer James O'Donnell is on top, and an unknown performer is on the right.

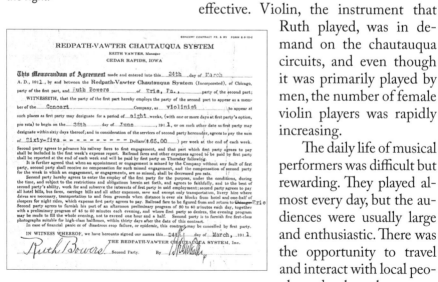

Ruth's 1911 contract with Redpath-Vawter.

The musical acts were selected for their ability and for how they fit into the mix of musical groups on a particular circuit. Groups usually had independence in their musical selection. The only exception was Sunday performances, in which the managers encouraged the incorporation of religious or sacred music into the program.

The size of the chautauqua stage and the amount of traveling made it difficult to accommodate large bands or orchestras, and there were only a few, like Thaviu's International Band or Kryl's Bohemian Band, who were successful on the chautauqua circuit. Groups like quartets or small ensembles were best suited to the chautauqua stage. The small size of most musical groups meant that the music, particularly classical music, had to be adapted, since there were usually only a few musical instruments. For singing groups, music that was suitable for a small number of voices was most effective. Violin, the instrument that Ruth played, was in demand on the chautauqua circuits, and even though it was primarily played by men, the number of female violin players was rapidly increasing.

The daily life of musical performers was difficult but rewarding. They played almost every day, but the audiences were usually large and enthusiastic. There was the opportunity to travel and interact with local people and other chautauqua performers. For musicians like Ruth, the morning usually started with a train trip to the town where they would play that day. Generally, the ride was under two hours. When they arrived at their destination, their baggage would be transported to the hotel where they were staying. Since they were traveling for at least a few months and had dress clothes for their stage performances, most people brought large steamer trunks.

This is from a postcard that Gibby sent to Ruth on her 1911 tour. It was addressed to her and named her recital company. Gibby included two possible locations, Perry and Newton. Initially the postcard went to Perry (stamped on top) and from there was sent to Newton, where it was received as general delivery on the morning of July 28. Ruth picked up the card when she arrived in Newton the following day.

Once they checked into their hotel, they would usually go to the post office to pick up any mail sent to them via general delivery. Performers would give their tour dates and locations to family and friends, who would send mail to a town a few days in advance of their arrival so that it would be waiting for them. Then it would be time for lunch, practice and preparation for the afternoon program. After the performance, they had a few hours of free time. This provided an opportunity to take a walk, visit a local attraction, do an activity with other chautauqua performers or visit someone in town who had invited them to their place. Following supper and the evening performance, there was sometimes a special community activity before it was time for bed.

Ruth's contract with the Redpath-Vawter Chautauqua for 1911 provided for a payment of sixty-five dollars per week, a large salary at that time. Redpath-Vawter also paid for her transportation between towns. However, Ruth had considerable expenses. There was the daily cost of a hotel room and meals, as well as keeping performance clothes neat and clean and numerous incidental expenses.

By the time Ruth performed on her first lyceum and chautauqua tours in 1910, the format of the programs had been established and they were just starting to achieve the success and popularity that would make them a well-known part of American culture during the next two decades of the twentieth century.

RUTH BOWERS

Ruth Bowers was born on June 4, 1888, in Erie, Pennsylvania, the first child of George and Cora Bowers. Ruth's maternal grandfather, D.P. Robbins, was a Civil War veteran, physician, newspaper editor and real estate speculator, among his many adventures. D.P. believed that his daughters should have the same opportunity for education as his sons, so Cora and her younger sister, Helena, completed high school. Both also received further education, an infrequent occurrence in the late nineteenth century. Cora attended art school in Erie so that she could pursue her passion for painting and develop her talent, while Helena trained to be a teacher.

Ruth's paternal grandfather, Jonas Bowers, was prominent in the construction industry in Erie, and George became a stationary engineer. However, by the time Ruth was in her early teens, George quit this work and became his wife's business agent, for Cora's art career was successful enough to provide sufficient income for the family. George also took on most of the domestic work, a rarity for men at that time.

Music was an important part of the Bowers family life. Cora was an accomplished pianist, while George played the clarinet, performed in local bands and was a founding member of the Erie Musicians' Union. Ruth began playing the violin when she was four and quickly demonstrated talent with that instrument. Her younger brother, Everett, played the cello. The family spent many evenings practising in the parlor, and in the summer, when the windows were open, neighbors frequently stopped outside to hear them play. When Ruth and Everett were in their early teens, George and Cora, along with a few other musicians, formed the Bowers Family Orchestra and performed locally. Ruth also began playing solos at concert programs in Erie.

After graduating from high school in 1906, Ruth wanted to become a professional violinist. She enrolled at the newly formed Pratt Institute in Pittsburgh, founded by Silas G. Pratt, an American composer who was the first person to set "America the Beautiful" to music. (Pratt's version is not the tune that is used today.) The institute offered

OPPOSITE PAGE: Ruth when she was seven years old.

a scholarship in the violin department and Ruth won the competition. An Erie newspaper reported that she had "taken her first step towards the realization of the high hopes entertained for her by her many admirers and friends."[6] In succeeding years, the Erie newspapers frequently reported on Ruth's activities. Ruth spent two years at the Pratt Institute. While there, she studied with Franz Kohler, the first violinist with the Pittsburgh Symphony and one of the leading violinists of that era. During that time she played in many local musical programs. At one of these she met Charles Gibson, a young man from Pittsburgh who would become her husband. She graduated in 1908 as the first concert violinist from Pratt Institute.

Ruth returned to Erie for the summer of 1908 but came back to Pittsburgh that fall. During the next year, she played in the Pittsburgh area, as well as in some programs in Erie. She also had the opportunity to play at a few venues with the Elma B. Smith Company during their lyceum tour of northern Pennsylvania in 1909.

Ruth's determination to have a career as a violinist finally attained success in January 1910, when she obtained the position of first violinist with the Ramos Spanish Orchestra as they prepared for a winter lyceum tour through the American Midwest. The *Chicago Music News* wrote on January 14:

> The Ramos Orchestra, fresh from a very successful trip, has been in Chicago the last week preparing some new repertoire and rehearsing with some new soloists. Miss Ruth Bowers, violinist, was heard playing the *Zigeunerweisen* by Sarasate and the Schubert *Bee* in which she displayed a remarkably good musical quality and considerable facility. Miss Bowers is a native of Erie, Pa. and has studied extensively at Pittsburgh, and has played there repeatedly; as well as other concert points. Her engagement as soloist with the Ramos Orchestra constitutes the first in which she has played solo with such accompaniment. The Ramos Orchestra is the "head liner" of the Redpath Lyceum Bureau and has a very long tour for the balance of the season.[7]

OPPOSITE PAGE: Ruth as violinist before going on tour.

Sig. Fransasco Ramos

DIRECTOR

RAMOS SPANISH ORCHESTRA

THE RAMOS SPANISH ORCHESTRA
JANUARY — MARCH 1910

The Ramos Spanish Orchestra spent the fall of 1909 on a lyceum tour through Ohio, Indiana and Illinois. Franasco Ramos was the director and played the clarinet. The orchestra included singer Frederic Irving; Antonio Regina, who played the cornet; and five women who played the violin, cello and piano. The members wore costumes that emphasized the Spanish theme. The orchestra played to full houses on the lyceum circuit and received glowing newspaper reviews. Ramos, by all accounts, was a brilliant musician. Unfortunately, he had a temperamental personality and did not get along with the other members of the orchestra.

Not long after the tour started, the Redpath-Slayton Lyceum Bureau began receiving letters of complaint. Ramos and Irving did not get along and each wrote detailed letters denouncing the other person to Harry Harrison, the manager for the lyceum. Some of the women wrote protesting Ramos's treatment and his attempts to fine them for supposed infractions, and a couple of them threatened to quit. The mother of one of the women wrote to the lyceum protesting Ramos's treatment of her daughter. Even members of the public commented to the lyceum about Ramos's performance.

After a program in Bushnell, Illinois, the secretary of the organizing committee told the lyceum:

> In my estimation Mr. Ramos is a weak point in the organization. While I like the vim and dash he puts into his directing there are times where it borders on the freakish and attracts too much attention entirely. Kindly allow me to suggest how to make this organization a world beater—get a new director.

A church pastor from Galesburg, Illinois, sent a letter to Harrison after the orchestra's performance there. He noted that there was "much

OPPOSITE PAGE: Señor Ramos in an official Redpath-Slayton portrait. Redpath Chautauqua Collection, University of Iowa.

of merit in the concert itself and the individual performers gave excellent satisfaction." But he was critical of Ramos's performance:

> The man who is supposed to be the star, the conductor Ramos, came as near spoiling the whole attraction as could well be. His manner in conducting an orchestra of half a dozen would fill Creatore[†] with an orchestra of one hundred with envy. His gymnastics were wonderful to behold. I think everyone in the audience of real musical understanding and appreciation, and of such there are many in Galesburg, was certainly disappointed. As a conductor Ramos is freakish, even absurd. He undoubtedly is an excellent musician, understanding the compositions thoroughly, but he does not understand an American audience nor does he show the difference between intensity and excessive manifestation of idiosyncrasy as to attract announced attention to himself at the expense of the real merit of the orchestra or the soloists.

A musician commented:

> I think it is a splendid company with one exception. Mr. Ramos really kills the whole performance with his never ending gyrations and gesticulation, and the stuff he puts on is unworthy of your backing and in my candid opinion the sooner you let him go the better it would be for you.

On December 13, Harry Harrison wrote to Ramos:

> We have decided that after the holidays we will send a manager with the orchestra from the bureau and he will have complete charge and direct for us. This is a great additional expense, for we had not counted on it, but we are certainly tired of the continual scrapping of Mr. Irving and yourself. Frankly, I think both of you are to blame...I think you are wrong many times in treating the girls haughtily.

At the Christmas break, all but one of the women left, so Ramos had to replace most of the orchestra. The *Chicago Music News* described the new members:

---

† Giuseppe Creatore was a famous Italian band leader in the early twentieth century who was known for his flamboyant style of conducting. He and his band performed on the chautauqua circuit for several years. Several people mentioned that Ramos's conducting was similar to Creatore's style.

Sr. Ramos carries in his organization an ensemble of prize medal musicians among whom may be mentioned Miss Ethel Freeman, diamond medalist of the Chicago Musical College, Lillian Brockway, who received two medals from the Chicago Musical College, Miss Rosalie Jacobsohn, the well-known concert cellist, and daughter of Mr. Jacobsohn, late concert master of Theodore Thomas' orchestra, and other not less prominent artists.

The *News* also mentioned Ruth Bowers.

The Spanish poet-conductor believes Miss Bowers has a great future before her and compares her exceptional talent to that of the greatest artists of the day. Her tone work is remarkable for its breadth and enormous quality, and the technical difficulties of her extensive repertoire are accomplished with great ease.[8]

Whether Ruth knew of the difficulties that the Spanish Orchestra had during the fall is unknown. Certainly the opportunity to expand her musical career and travel were key considerations for accepting the offer. Ruth's parents supported her decision to play on the lyceum circuit. She had spent three years in Pittsburgh and had traveled on a few short tours regionally. Now she would develop her talent by playing to a wider audience.

Ramos' Spanish Orchestra

NO brief announcement can do justice to Ramos' Spanish Orchestra. It stands on a plane of excellence so far above other musical organizations of its class that no mere word-picture, however cleverly phrased, can give more than a faint idea of its true merits. Its playing has been a revelation to the music world. Every instrument is controlled by a master hand; producing cloud-bursts of harmonious tones that make the blood tingle, quicken the pulse, stir the imagination, and wield an irresistible influence on the emotions.

Señor Franasco Ramos, director of the company, is a new figure of force and power in the concert field. Before entering upon his present career he was bandmaster of the 12th United States Cavalry, where he won distinction as a musician of the highest type. He has all of Creatore's dash and spirit on the director's stand, with an abundance of fire and magnetism that is all his own. Wherever he appears with his orchestra he leaps into immediate popularity. Not only is he a great musical director, but he is also a specialist on the clarionet, an instrument which he has developed and perfected until its wonderful possibilities, heretofore half-hidden, have been fully realized. What Paganini did for violin the genius of Franasco Ramos has done for the clarionet. He is the inventor of the Ramos system for that instrument, which has greatly enchanced its importance and value as a musical medium.

The concerts given by the Ramos Spanish Orchestra are made up of classical and popular selections in sufficient variety to delight any audience. A pleasing feature of every program is the singing of Mr. Frederic Irving, the celebrated baritone whose repeated triumphs in grand opera roles have given him a standing among the great artists of the day. Mr. Irving was the leading man in the Schumann-Heink rendition of "Love's Lottery" and many other successes, no less brilliant, stand to his credit. He has a clear, resonant voice of wonderful range and quality, which rises above the orchestra accompaniment with imposing effect.

This description comes from the Redpath-Slayton Lyceum bureau brochure.

At the end of December, Ruth traveled to Chicago, where she stayed at the home of her mother's cousin Vella Moll. The Ramos Spanish Orchestra spent a week in the city rehearsing before departing on the winter tour on January 7. While traveling on the train, Ruth wrote in a letter to her mother: "The girls are perfectly lovely. We are all strangers and have been getting acquainted...They are all in their twenties, all well-educated, both musically and in school, and are all out to save some money so I think we will get along fine." She noted: "We each carry suitcases & then there are two great property trunks in which we are going to put all our extras. Really the suits are very pretty—black velvet skirts, yellow silk blouses & black velvet boleros, little yellow silk caps & red slippers & stockings (we buy the slippers and stockings)." Ruth also commented that "the orchestra music is very hard and it keeps me hustling to get over it. I haven't had much time to practice it."

The Ramos Spanish Orchestra, accompanied by Julius Rohde, the manager sent by the Redpath-Slayton Lyceum, gave their first program at Northwood, Iowa, on January 8. After the concert Rohde wrote to Harrison: "The new people took their places in the company very nicely and made it better." The orchestra then spent a week at venues in Minnesota. On January 13, from Sandstone, Rohde wrote Harrison about the progress of the tour:

> I find Ramos a hard fellow to get along with. I can usually get along with decent people but he and I have had several mix-ups and he won't be decent. We have had several bad mix-ups because I would not stand his abuse. He was much better today...I simply have to keep him and Mr. Irving apart to avoid quarrels between them and now have their wardrobes in separate trunks.

Ramos also wrote to Harrison on the same day.

> This is to report to you that things are OK with Mr. Irving, until the other fellow came along, but now both sympathize, and the troubles are worse than before, because there is two now instead of one. However, I will try to overcome as many troubles as possible. If you can just make them understand emphatically that my orchestra must be left alone, no chaperoning is allowed strictly.

OPPOSITE PAGE: The Ramos Spanish Orchestra's 1909–10 program.

BULLETIN --- PROGRAM

THE REDPATH LYCEUM BUREAU

PRESENTS

Ramos Spanish Orchestra

AND

Mr. Frederick Irving, Soloist

Tour of 1909-1910

Sr. Franasco Ramos, Director................................Clarinetist
Frederic Irving...Bass-Baritone
Ruth Bowers..First Violin
Eva Odell...First Violin
Maud Woollett...Second Violin
A. Regina...Cornetist
Rosalie Jacobsohn..'Cello
Lilliau Brockway...Piano

SOLOISTS

Frederic Irving...Bass-Baritone
Ruth Bowers...Violiniste
A. Regina...Cornetist
Lillian Brockway...Accompanist

PROGRAM

1. March—Carmen..Bizet
2. Overture--William Tell...................................Rossini
3. Toreador Song—Carmen.................................Bizet
   Mr. Irving and Orchestra
4. Columbia—For Cornet.................................Liberati
5. Selections from Pagliacci.........................Leoncavallo
   Introducing: "Prologue," "Tempo de Minuetto,"
   "Nedda to the Butterflies," "Laugh of Pagliacci,"
   "Tempo de Gavotta," "When You Will Be Acting
   the Fool," and the "All Forgot" song
6. (a) Charity.......................................⎫
   (b) Fulfillment....................................⎬ Jas. G. MacDermid
   (c) Love's Great Song...........................⎭
   Mr. Irving
7. Oh! You Girls— Polka..............................Franasco Ramos
8. Concerto—Melodias Gitanas.........................Sarasate
   Miss Ruth Bower, Orchestral Accompaniment
9. American Patrol.....................................Meacham
10. Selection from Il Trovatore..........................Verdi
    Introducing: "Anvil Chorus," "Gipsy Song," "Duet"
    from Third Act, "Cavatina" from First Act,
    "Miserere"

Harry Harrison replied to Ramos: "Glad that everything is going along smoothly with you. Trust that you will make it pleasant for Mr. Rohde, as he is a mighty nice fellow."

The Montevideo Leader described the program by the Ramos Spanish Orchestra on January 15:

A SPLENDID CONCERT

The concert given at the Opera House last Saturday night by Ramos' Spanish Orchestra, assisted by Mr. Frederic Irving, baritone soloist, was certainly one of the very best ever given before a Montevideo audience. Senor Ramos is a genius in his ability to bring out all the music there is in his orchestra and in his splendid selections. He had his players completely under his control all the time and they being true artists, responded splendidly to his leadership.

There were five ladies in the orchestra: two first violinists, second violinist, cellist and pianist, also Mr. A. Regina, a very fine cornetist, besides the director who played the clarinet. The selections were all of the classic order and each was rendered with splendid effect. The Orchestra appeared in pretty Spanish costumes. Mr. Irving first appeared in a like costume singing the Toreador song with fine effect. He also sang three other numbers and responded to a hearty encore. He has a magnificent voice and added much to the entertainment. Mr. Regina gave a beautiful cornet solo and Miss Ruth Bowers, leading violinist,

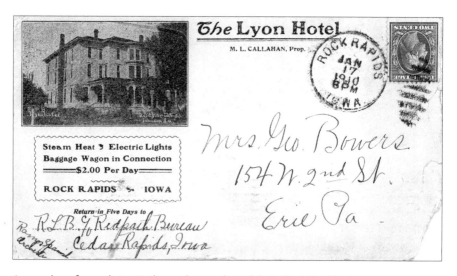

An envelope from a letter Ruth sent her mother while in Rock Rapids, Iowa.

gave a splendid violin solo showing her wonderful control of that wonderful instrument, and giving herself up completely to her highest ideals of the piece. Answering an enthusiastic and appreciative encore she gave "My Old Kentucky Home" in perfect duet, and without a flaw, the shadings being as delicate and perfect as we ever heard. The concert was patronized by a large and appreciative audience and all were delighted with it.[9]

From Montevideo, Minnesota, the orchestra traveled to Rock Rapids, Iowa, where they performed on January 17. At the Lyon Hotel, Ruth wrote to her mother, describing the tour.

In my letter Saturday I guess I didn't tell you anything about Montevideo. It's a dandy place, very hilly and some beautiful homes there, about 2500 inhabitants. The concert was given at the opera house to a crowded house again and it went fine, and again I made a big hit and had to bow twice after "Kentucky Home." You said it was funny such small places paid such big salaries for attractions. It isn't when you consider that the course is the event of the winter and in many places this is the only musical event and the admissions have been 75 cents in almost every town and never less than 50 cents.

Yesterday Mr. Rohde & I went to church (Methodist) and oh! What a fuss they made over me after the services. Many of them told me my solo was by far the best thing on the whole program.

After church back to the hotel for dinner and we got paid. Oh! How nice to receive two twenty dollar bills. I have just sent $10 to [Franz] Kohler and am going to the P.O. to send $15 to you. Will try and send you that each week and after the $40 I borrowed has been paid, then pay my bill at Fulmers and Wilson. After I've sent enough to pay those I'll tell you what to do with the rest.

After dinner we took the train for Granite Falls and got there at 4 o'clock, went to a hotel and we all went to bed. Stayed there till 12:30 when we took a train to Sioux Falls, S.D. Got there at 7 this morn, got breakfast and again to bed till 12 o'clock. Got up and got my dinner and took the train here arriving at 3:15. So you see my sleep is pretty broken up, but I make it up as much as possible. We have had some pretty big jumps to make but I don't mind it, in fact I rather enjoy it except those fierce night rides.

We have a hard ride tomorrow, in fact we may have to leave tonight as the trains are late on the account of a snow storm and we may not make connections by waiting till tomorrow…

I must go to the Post Office and then come back & practice. Tell Everett to write. I really have so little time to do writing.

From Rock Rapids in northwestern Iowa, the orchestra proceeded to South Dakota for a few concerts. Mechanical trouble with a train caused them to miss their scheduled engagement at Elk Point. The local newspaper described the situation:

> The Ramos Spanish orchestra people were stranded at Yankton all the afternoon and evening Thursday, not being able to reach Elk Point until 11 p.m., the afternoon passenger from the west being over seven hours late. We were kept in touch with them by telephone and not until after 8 o'clock was the concert abandoned. Arrangements were made and announced for a matinee Friday afternoon, which under the circumstance, was the best the management could do.
>
> All holders of season tickets, and as many others as possible, were notified by telephone and a full audience gathered at 3 o'clock and enjoyed one of the best musical treats ever heard in Elk Point. The program was varied and exacting, embracing everything from national airs to the most classical compositions. Among the latter were selections from Carmen, William Tell, Pagliacci and Verdi's *Il Trovatore*. Frederick Irving, the bass baritone, had a magnificent voice notable for its range and power. The cornetist, A. Regina, did himself and the management credit. Special note should be given Miss Ruth Bowers, the first violinist. She executed the "Melodias Gitanas" of Sarasate's Concerto with such appreciation and effect that she was given a hearty encore. "My Old Kentucky Home" was never played with more expression than by her on the recall. Very rarely if ever has the music loving public of Elk Point heard better orchestral talent, here or elsewhere, than that presented last Friday afternoon in the third number of our Lyceum course.[10]

In late January, trouble started in the Ramos Spanish Orchestra. After Elk Point the orchestra performed in Kingsley, Iowa, on January 22. Some people in the community enjoyed the orchestra so much that they tried to arrange for a church concert, since the orchestra had an open date on Sunday, January 23. Unfortunately, Ramos's fee was too high for them. Frederic Irving, Ruth Bowers and Lillian Brockway decided that they would perform for the people at a very reasonable fee. The Kingsley newspaper described the event:

A Most Delightful Musical

A union meeting of the churches of Kingsley was held at the Congregational church last Sunday evening and the services were conducted by Miss Ruth Bowers, first violinist, Lillian Brockway, pianist and Frederic Irving, bass baritone soloist of the Ramos Spanish Orchestra. The program was listened to by about 500 people and was greatly enjoyed by all. Mr. Irving pronounced it one of the most attentive congregations they have ever appeared before. Following is the program as rendered at the churches:

Opened by hymn by congregation and prayer by Rev. Taylor of the M.E. church,

1. "The Lost Chord"   Sullivan
2. "The Lord is My Light"   Allitsen
3. Cavatina   Raff
4. "O! Dry Those Tears"   Del Riego
5. *Träumerei* (Dream'd)   Schumann
   (also Adagio by Ole Bull: listed with 5)
6. "The Peace of God"   Gounod
7. Humoresque   Dvorak
   (also Andante by Wienjoroska: listed with 7)
8. "Mother O' Mine"   Kipling tours
   (also "Rosary" by Nevin; listed with 8)
9. "The Holy City"   Adonis
10. "Palm Branches"   Faure

Miss Bowers has toured the east a number of times and her work on the violin shows that she is a musician of the highest rank and the melody produced on the instrument was marvelous. She was ably assisted by Lillian Brockway on the piano. Mrs. Brockway is also a musician of extreme merit and holds a number of splendid medals for her work on the piano. Mr. Frederic Irving, bass soloist has a wonderful voice and rendered a number of beautiful sacred selections...

It was hoped by our people to have the entire orchestra participate in this service but Prof. Ramos' price was so high that it was beyond reach and Miss Bowers, Mrs. Brockway and Mr. Irving consented to render the program for a guarantee, which we understand, so angered Prof. Ramos that he made threats to discharge Miss Bowers and Mrs. Brockway if they participated in the service Sunday evening, but the ladies were not to be frightened and the program was carried through.[11]

Rohde wrote to Harrison the following day.

Ramos is raising the devil again. He has telegraphed to Chicago
for another violinist and received a favorable reply. It is all because Miss Bowers played at church last night by request of the
committee of people there. At first he was in favor of it and then
asked Mr. Irving to sing and later tried to stop it, after it had been
announced in all the churches.

Miss Bowers is fine and the one who makes the hit with the
people and we cannot afford to lose anyone who wins favor for
us as she does. Can you wire him not to change? I have written
Mr. Vawter and tried to telephone him but he is gone. I tried to
reason with Ramos but he wants to change two girls. It would be
a shame as they all work together so nicely and please the people
so well. A change will be very injurious in the least to the bureau,
and there is no sense in it…

Ramos is jealous of his own people. They receive too much
applause to suit him, while he appears ridiculous and amuses the
people.

Hastily,
Julius H. Rohde

Do try to head off Ramos if you can. I'll try again.

Ramos wrote to Harrison on January 25, complaining about the special program. He told him:

A committee of people came and asked me if I could give an
extra sacred concert at the church. I made my price, but then
Irving came and gave another price, promising that he would hire
the soloists, as he did. This put me in trouble, and obliged me to
perhaps fire two of the girls. If the Bureau will not help me I will
have to get rid of him in some way. He introduces the girls always
to undesirable parties.

Ramos also sent a telegram to Harrison the next day, telling him,
"Cannot stand Irving any longer. Will substitute him to any expense."

On the same day that Ramos wrote his letter, Julius Rohde provided
a detailed explanation of the situation to Harrison after the concert at
Correctionville on January 24. The manager stated:

Ramos discharged Miss Bowers last evening before the concert, but she made a few threats to him about her contract and he backed down and re-engaged her. Then he discharged Mrs. Brockway, pianist, and told her to go home tomorrow. She then refused to play for the evening concert and the other girls joined her in refusal. It looked at 7 o'clock as though the company was disrupted but they finally all agreed to go on and Mrs. Brockway stays for the present. Ramos tells them he has two others engaged for their places…

Rohde was exasperated:

I don't understand the fellow. I thought I had him under control but see I am mistaken. I think that you better send him word that the Bureau wants no more changes made in the orchestra because it is liable to ruin the whole thing. All work together so nicely

'Neath the Pines: Frederic Irving gave Ruth this postcard in Correctionville, Iowa. "My Dear Miss Bowers—No doubt you will always remember this town and its most appropriate name, as several things in your experience with Sr. Fr. Ramos were corrected here. Whenever you wander among the pines or 'neath them you will doubtless think of our snowy cold trip way up here, where we 'just come from the pole.' If you ever take a lunch "neath the pines' in dear old Penn[sylvania] don't fail to serve cocoa in remembrance."

now and there was no reason why he should discharge them, only as he said he felt humiliated that they played at the church after he objected.

In closing, Rohde noted that "the concerts are giving splendid satisfaction."

Rohde also sent a follow-up telegram to Harrison: "Ramos incorrigible. Wire him a settler. Irving and girls absolutely all right."

Two days later Rohde wrote another detailed letter to Harrison and declared that "the man [Ramos] is surely crazy." Ramos had hired replacements for Bowers and Brockway but Rohde, as manager, told him that he had to retain the two ladies. "He had to get angry at someone and this time it was Irving." Rohde continued:

Now he threatens not to play for Irving and at Marcus tried to stop the orchestra from playing the part for the Toreador song, but the girls did it anyway. He has now written for another singer which he proposes to put in place for Mr. Irving. He, Ramos, made some threats about cutting his throat, and sent word to the girls by Regina that he was about to do something that might cause his [Regina] going to the police station. I think he is going mad.

Rohde noted that "aside from him there is perfect harmony and [it] is the most congenial crowd a fellow can find. The orchestra is still together but no telling how long." He continued, "The program can be given without him. We know, as we gave most of it without him at Springfield, S.D. [South Dakota] when he refused to ride with us on that drive."

Harrison initially advised Rohde, "Let Ramos have complete control and when anything is to be said or done regarding the orchestra, refer it all to Ramos. He is responsible, and if anything goes wrong deduct it from his salary or write me about it and I will write him or instruct you to deduct from his salary."

On January 28 Harrison replied to Ramos:

I am sure things will be all straightened up before you get this letter and that everything will be running on smoothly again. Do not make any more changes than you have to, although this is up to you, as we are counting on you to go ahead and do the right thing. I think though, Ramos, you get a little too jealous of the company when they want to play in churches. That helps you, it helps the company, and helps the bureau.

He also reminded Ramos: "Regarding Irving, we have a contract with him which we cannot break, and furthermore he is advertised on the circular as soloist and we must carry out this year's agreement."

Irving got involved in the conflict too. On January 27 he wrote a letter to Harrison explaining his use of the ladies' dressing room.

Having a voice to keep in shape and having to sit in thin clothing during the greater part of the program, somewhere, I have used the ladies' dressing room, to make my two changes of costume in, except when the gentlemen's dressing room has been warm which has been very seldom. My first number being the third on the program I do not need to go near that dressing room, and do not do so, until the ladies are on the platform playing their first number. I make my two changes and sit near the heat in the dressing room only when the ladies do not need it for they are on the platform playing. I change back into my street clothes, packing my costumes and putting them in the trunk, removing everything from the dressing room at the beginning of their last number and do not return to the dressing room at all. I have to be at the back of the audience to sing in the last number. I have done this same way since we started out in October and not until last night did Mr. Ramos ever ask me not to do so.

The ladies sent a supporting letter signed by all of them:

This is to certify that on our first evening at Northwood, Iowa, Mr. Irving asked all of the ladies of the Ramos Spanish Orchestra if we had any objection to his using our dressing room after we were through with it and while we did not need it. We all replied that we certainly had no objection. And we wish to again say that we still have no objection, as he is entirely gentlemanly in the use of it, and does not disturb us in any way.

From Goldfield, on January 28, Ramos sent a telegram to Harrison:

"I have my own manager, thirty five dollars [weekly]. Discharge Rohde immediately. Irving will be alright for the season." At the end of the telegram Ramos warned: "Answer to Garner [Iowa] or this means legal resignation." Two days later Ramos wrote a letter to Harrison reiterating his desire to have a new manager.

"To Miss Ruth Bowers. With many pleasant memories of the Spanish Orchestra and you. Sincerely—Frederic Irving as 'The Toreador' in *Carmen*."

"I don't want to make you lose money by stopping the orchestra or change the manager without giving you a full explanation of my situation, then if you don't protect me it will mean you have change your good will you have had to me." Ramos also stated, "the orchestra now is the best I ever had."

Rohde sent a letter of explanation on the same day. He believed that the fault for the discord in the orchestra belonged to the conductor.

No one can get along with Ramos even by giving up to him. The same trouble would exist with anyone. Whatever Irving's faults are he has been a gentleman since I have been with the company and I think that all the girls will bear me out in this statement. Ramos simply falsifies to you…I am not taking his [Irving's] part, but he has been accommodating.

Rohde refuted Ramos's contention about Irving's conduct with the ladies.

The girls are not being introduced to any undesirable parties, but often we cannot help introduce them to our committee when they want to get acquainted with our people. This is no more than courtesy to them…All the trouble so far has been caused by Ramos. Nearly every day he has to take his ugly spite out on someone, and all for nothing…Several times he has tried to spoil Irving's singing…[T]he secret of the orchestra's success is in excellent musicians of which it is composed, and at Springfield [South Dakota], when Ramos refused to go on the drive with us, the program was carried out quite successfully under Regina's direction. Ramos came on train about 9:30 and finished it up…[Ramos] has threatened me several times but his threats spell nothing with me, and I'll not be bluffed.

Rohde noted that Maud Woollett, who played second violin, had left the orchestra and been replaced by Mabel Kellogg. He commented:

I suppose he will send in other reports of these occurrences to you and you can look at it again from his angle of view. I am writing you this rather elaborate report merely to show you the truth in the matter…If it were not that I am anxious to save this business for Mr. Vawter and for my loyalty to him I'd not have humored

Ramos as much as I have or strained every effort to hold this company together.

Despite the turmoil backstage, the concerts continued to be success-ful and were praised in the local newspapers. The *Correctionville News* reported:

> It has been a long time since the people of this community have been so pleased with a public event as they were with the con-cert given at the opera house Monday evening by the Ramos Spanish orchestra, assisted by the distinguished bass-baritone, Frederic Irving. The number was the fourth in the local enter-tainment course and season ticket holders realized that in that one event they got their money's worth...The audience Mon-day evening practically filled the opera house and throughout the excellent program the keenest enjoyment was had and the audience was not backward in showing its pleasure.[12]

From Correctionville the orchestra proceeded to Marcus and then to Pomeroy, where the editor of the *Pomeroy Herald* stated:

> Writing under the inspiration of the pleasure derived from hearing the Ramos Spanish Orchestra last evening it is difficult to limit comment to the space which governs its value as a news item. To say that the program pleased is putting it mildly. The largest crowd attending any of the course numbers had been attracted to this concert and every patron was delighted. Senor Ramos is a forceful director, capable of commanding from his accomplished players the effects that he desired. He is demon-strative, but every motion is the expression of a musical spirit. He was not heard in a clarinet solo, so it is impossible to judge of his capability as a performer, but he is surely a forceful direc-tor of artistic music...[13]

Ruth wrote from Garner on January 29.

Dear Mama,
    Such excitement! The plot thickens! Enter villain, etc.
    Really, I don't know whether I can tell you the events of the past few days! A regular nightmare, altho it hasn't concerned me at all, but to be witness to so much trouble—oh never again!
    Mr. Ramos has acted like a dirty sneak the past week, hasn't spoken to any of us, etc, fights with the manager, threatens to

choke Mr. Irving, etc, but the climax was reached yesterday when upon our arrival here (Garner) lo and behold a new violinist loomed up. Imagine our feelings—all of us wondered which one was to be discharged but we were kept in suspense till yesterday eve after the concert when Mr. Ramos (Sinner as Mr. Rohde calls him) told Miss Wollett, the 2nd violinist to pack up and leave— result of which a lawyer has been flying around here and every-thing is in a hub-bub. Just when things were going so smoothly, the orchestra was going like clockwork and now he wants Miss Odell to play 2nd violin (and she knows the 1st parts perfectly and we get along so nice together) and the new girl to play 2nd first, and they are so hard I just see where it will be lovely.

Oh, I am so disgusted with the whole thing. We all wanted to go on a strike last eve but here's hoping things will get straight-ened out. I have such a constant headache from this awful discord.

We girls all get along beautifully but the men—oh—it's aw-ful. We all stick up for Rohde and of course that makes Sinner furious.

Thursday you should have seen us at a station called Eagle Grove. We had a six mile drive so of course Mr. Rohde as man-ager went ahead to get the best rigs he could for us which he did: three rigs—two two-seated cutters for us girls—Eva, Mr. Regina & driver and I in one, the other 3 girls & driver in the other, Mr. Rohde, Mr. Irving & baggage in a bobsleigh—but listen to this. At exactly the time those rigs drove up—along comes Ramos with the worst looking bob and demands that we all go with him. We all sat like a lot of bumps on logs. Mr. Rohde said to go with him and he would see that things were OK. Then a fight proceeded—oh joy, right in the station. Imag-ine our feelings—but the dear only knows what will happen next. But I'll stick to the last as everybody has been very nice to me and I have had no trouble myself.

I am sorry to say that I had a little siege of sickness Wednes-day night, I felt miserable, Thursday worse, ached in every square inch of my body, sore throat and just felt awful. As soon as we got to Fort Dodge where we changed at noon, I went to a physi-cian who informed me I had a very bad case of tonsillitis and if I wasn't better next day to go to bed & stay there. Had a fever of 101 and such a backache I could hardly stand up. Imagine how I felt to play, but the doctor gave me gargle and tablets for the ache and the girls fixed up hot lemonade and I took a hot foot bath and I'm thankful to say I feel pretty good today altho sort of weak as today I have eaten my first mouthful for over two days. Been living on hot milk.

Ruth also wrote about the difficulties they were having getting to their next venue.

Payday tomorrow but horrors we will miss our date tonight and consequently miss our pay...Just think, we are to leave here at 9 o'clock this morn and the train isn't here yet (1:45). Mr. Rohde is trying to get a special for us but can't and I suppose we will be dumped off at some hole to stay all day tomorrow. But we are to start for Canton anyhow and it remains to be seen where we land.

Despite the turmoil within the orchestra, the members continued to give fine programs. The newspaper in Garner provided detailed coverage of the concert in their town.

RAMOS' SPANISH ORCHESTRA

The opera house was crowded last Friday night to hear Ramos' Spanish orchestra. Lovers of music expected to hear something good but were not quite prepared for the rare musical feast they enjoyed. As a musical production we liked this the best of any we have heard in Garner. Each instrument was in the hands of an artist and Prof. Ramos displayed rare skill in harmonizing and bringing out the proper parts so as to be most pleasing to the ear. Ruth Bowers played a violin solo with orchestral accompaniment so beautiful that she had to respond to an encore when she gave us "My Old Kentucky Home" in double stop and played so divinely sweet that we wished it would have lasted all night. Rosalie Jacobsohn did some excellent work on the cello. The cornetist was heavily encored. He is an artist and did some fine work in triple tongue. Lillian Brockway, the pianist, is an artist of exquisite skill and Eva Odell and Susan Hammond both did excellent work on their parts.

The orchestra itself made a rare evening's entertainment but it was just doubled by the additional feature of Frederic Irving's singing. Mr. Irving has a voice of a great power and rare sweetness, a combination not usual in public singers. Add to this excellent skill and soul singing instead of mouth singing and you may judge the rare treat it was to hear him sing. He just can't help singing beautifully.[14]

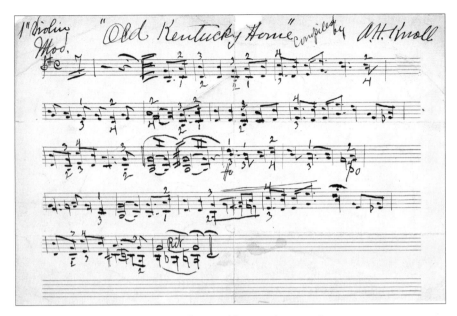

Ruth regularly played this version of "My Old Kentucky Home" as an encore.

The orchestra spent the end of January and the beginning of February playing in communities in northern Iowa and southern Minnesota. At Plainview, Minnesota, Ramos wrote to Harrison, once more trying to fire Rohde.

> We lost date last Saturday and I blame Manager for it, so I had to pay in full to my orchestra. Waiting for your opinion on that point. He [Rohde] lost his suitcase yesterday in the train. Today he let the baggage go to some wrong station and at present I don't know where he is…I have engaged a new manager which will start next Monday.

Ramos also asked Harrison to send the train schedules for their travel and the contacts for each town. Harrison immediately replied:

> We do not have the itineraries, railroad schedules, etc. for the time in the west. These are in the Cedar Rapids office. Anything you do regarding manager will have to be taken up with that office. They have Mr. Rohde on a yearly salary so his time costs them nothing extra. I do not want to get into any of the mix-ups whatever, and I am simply refusing to have anything to do with it. We have a contract and I believe you will live up to it. I have never

found a man yet when I said I could trust him that ever went back on me. This is the reason I did not worry about your telegrams and letters for I thought you would do the right thing.

From Plainview the orchestra returned to Iowa for a concert at Hopkinton on February 4 and Walcott on February 5. During the train ride between the two towns, they went through Cedar Rapids. Ruth sent a postcard of the Montrose Hotel to her mother. "This is a grand hotel—where we had dinner today. Have been here over two hours. Met Mr. Vawter, the Redpath man, here."

The Ramos Spanish Orchestra had a day of rest at Davenport on Sunday, February 6, and Ruth wrote to her mother about the events of the week.

We have had a hard week traveling an awful lot. Oh, how we laugh when we get dressed at night. Miss Jacobsohn says she only has time to wash the right side of her face, as that is all that shows. Lillian took a bath at Austin, Minnesota the other day and said it was such a new experience she didn't know how to get in a real tub. Really Mama, it is fierce the way you have to hustle and get dressed in the morning and perhaps have no other opportunity to comb your hair all day, but after all it's enjoyable and I'm glad I came. Have seen so many places of interest and met so many nice people.

You ought to see me wash my clothes these days. Yesterday left a suit of underwear, nightgown and corset cover at the laundry to be delivered at Belle Plaines on Thurs., but I wash my own handkerchiefs & stockings. This eve I'm going to do a little washing, take a real bath and go to bed early.

Ruth noted that she had lost a day's pay because the orchestra did not get to Canton for their program. (This was the only engagement that the orchestra missed during their tour.) She also described their previous evening at Walcott.

Had a lovely supper served like a family party, we had a table all to ourselves and everything was put on and passed around. For the second time since I left Chicago I had jelly and canned pears. Oh, how I miss canned fruit, you must save a can of cherries for me when I get home.

But to go on about last night, I never in all my life played before such a crowd. The hall was crowded to the doors with people and it seemed to me about half the women had babies with them who kept up a continual performance. To add to the excitement a few dogs got in and would put up a howl every so often. The kids sat on the front benches and chewed peanuts and the men sat in the back and smoked. Oh, never again, but they seemed to enjoy it and applauded so that they could be heard above the uproar.

The Ramos Spanish Orchestra performed in Maquoketa on February 7. Here Ramos vented his anger and frustration, and this was reported in great detail in the *Maquoketa Excelsior*.

A NEW SPANISH WAR IS ON

Ramos' Orchestra Gives an Excellent Concert and Leader Furnishes Plenty of Excitement.

A large and enthusiastic audience greeted Ramos' Spanish Orchestra at the Opera House Monday evening, being quite the largest house which has attended of the Entertainment Course numbers. After a considerable delay the concert was begun and the audience enjoyed the splendid music little knowing of the exciting occurrences which almost resulted in the abandonment of the program entirely. Some perhaps noted that a swarthy, heavy set cornetist, evidently of Italian blood, led the players instead of the advertised Spaniard, whose instrument is the clarinet, but the playing was so finished — so beautiful that enthusiasm displaced curiosity and when the echoes of the final number had died away the people dispersed feeling that they had certainly received their money's worth. Mr. Irving, the baritone, also contributed much to the pleasure of the evening, the rotund tone, quality and power displayed in his singing being unusual in its excellence. One of his most pleasing numbers was one in which he suddenly commenced singing from the gallery, thus giving the audience a complete surprise.

Meanwhile a little comedy which was almost a tragedy was being enacted behind the scenes. During the day Mr. Ramos coolly informed Mr. Rickert that unless he was paid in advance there would be no concert. Mr. Rickert had been instructed by the Redpath Bureau to pay no money to Ramos, but to settle with Mr. Rohde, the Bureau's manager, who accompanied the troupe. This complicated matters. The time for the concert arrived, the orchestra assembled, but the doughty son of Hispania held the key to the situation and incidentally to the trunk in which all the music was kept. Followed arguful delay, until finally the local management served an ultimatum and then Mr. Rohde summoned assistance, and fell straightway upon Don Ramos and by force and violence relieved him of his keys, thereby relieving the situation. Mr. Rohde then appeared with the music, the fat cornetist took charge, and the program commenced while the deposed leader paced the floor in the rear of the stage and nursed his southern anger. Perhaps some of the audience may have noticed the frequent glances which the impromptu leader cast rearward over his shoulder These were born of a fear that Mr. Ramos might suddenly appear from the wings and perform a composition in sharps which was not on the printed program, said performance being executed with a knife which he was reputed to have concealed in his hosiery. But nothing occurred. Marshal Lockwood was called into action, and he and Manager Rohde kept watch over the tiger-like pacings of Mr. Ramos until the final note had died away into echoless silence. Then the second chapter commenced.

It appears that the Italian had purchased of Mr. Ramos a uniform for which he had agreed to pay $27.00 in weekly installments of $1.00 each. In chagrin over the episode of the leadership of his underling, Mr. Ramos had seized this uniform and when the purchaser heard of this purloining, his Italian blood surged into his head and the two mixed. A hot mix-up without reference to Queensbury rules or police regulations followed until Mr. Ramos pinned his adversary against the wall and to all appearances went seeking for his cutlery, when the Marshal went to bat and Mr. Ramos shortly discovered himself an inmate of the city bastille. This not being to his liking he produced coin of the realm in the sum of $25.00 as a bond for his appearance next morning and the incident closed. Tuesday morning he appeared before Justice House and parted with $5 and costs as a souvenir of Maquoketa's appreciation of his performance and the troupe departed for Tipton.[15]

R.J. Hammel, who operated a music school in Maquoketa and was one of the members of the town's lyceum committee, wrote to Keith Vawter:

Your company are ladies and gentlemen. Ramos, I believe, is a dope...He is, as I say, simply off, and a dangerous man to let loose. He has threatened the entire company. The show went big, the best number on the course. Regina played splendid—the violinist ditto—in fact the concert was a success...That they gave the splendid concert under strenuous conditions was wonder... Ramos is certainly bugs and should be pitied more than censured.

Antonio Regina.

Despite the turmoil Ramos created, the orchestra continued to provide excellent performances. The *Belle Plaine Democratic Herald* described the concert in their community on February 9, two days after Maquoketa.

RAMOS ORCHESTRA PLEASES

The Ramos Spanish Orchestra gave their concert at the Opera House Wednesday night to the usual Lecture Course Audience. They were decidedly the best organization of the kind heard in Belle Plaine for years. The seven [instruments], three violins, cello, cornet, piano, besides the clarinet played by the director, under the able leadership of Senor Ramos, made music that thrilled the audience and sallied forth rounds of applause after each number. Mr. Frederic Irving, who is with the company, has a powerful bass-baritone voice of wide range and the numbers were highly appreciated and he responded to encores each time in a pleasing manner.

Miss Ruth Bowers, the violin soloist, executed a selection and encore in a manner which won the admiration of all. Senor A. Regina, cornetist, also called forth applause in rendering "Columbia" in a very acceptable manner. One number by the Orchestra—"Oh You Girls" polka, composed by the director, Senor Ramos, made a decided hit and called forth another like selection. The last number on the program was selections from *Il Trovatore* and was the triumph of the evening's performance.

Many praises have been sung in favor of the organization and they are surely worthy of every favorable comment passed upon them.[16]

Ruth often used the expression "Oh you" in recognition of Señor Ramos's composition written for the ladies of the orchestra.

While traveling between Zearing and Winterset, Ruth had an opportunity to visit the state capitol in Des Moines. From there she sent a postcard to her brother, Everett. "Have been taking in the Capitol. Oh, it's great. Some handsome buildings here and it's a big place. Spent 2 hours at the Capitol. Went way up in the dome."

At Knoxville she sent a postcard to her boyfriend, Charles Gibson. "Where we are to play this eve. Many thanks for your remembrance of the 14th. We have had the dandiest weather out here until tonight, but it is getting awfully cold." In another postcard to her brother she wrote: "Am bumping along on a mixed train [freight and passengers] if you know what that is on my way to Monroe. Got up at 5 a.m. this morning. Ain't that grand?"

"Oh you Spaniard—Really, I didn't feel as tired as I looked."

"For all that is good Iowa affords the best. Sincerely, your friend, Julius H. Rohde." Traveling through Iowa during the winter. Julius Rohde is sitting in the middle. Ruth Bowers is standing behind and to the right of Rohde.

A few days later Ruth sent a postcard to Everett describing a weather phenomenon that was new to her. "The other day we saw a 'sun dog' and in the eve a big circle around the moon, both of which are considered bad weather signs but as yet nothing worse than a light snow storm here yesterday."

The performance at Burlington on February 19 was a special occasion for one member of the orchestra. The *Burlington Hawk Eye* reported that Frederic Irving, whose real name was William Frederic Irving Holcomb, had lived in Burlington for several years when he was a young man. "It proved a source of genuine delight to former old friends here, to note how this former Burlington singer had grown..." The newspaper reported that Irving was a native of nearby Mount Pleasant and a graduate of Elliott's Business College. "Mr. Irving was well received. He has a good stage presence and a pleasing voice of considerable range and power and he has that voice under perfect control. He won a host of friends here, who will be glad to see him again, early and often."[17]

Two nights later the orchestra played to a large audience in Keokuk. The newspaper produced a detailed account of this performance.

ALMOST PERFECT ORCHESTRATION

APPEARANCE OF THE RAMOS SPANISH ORCHESTRA

Third Number in YMCA Entertainment Course

Program is Perfectly Interpreted

Constituted One of the Most Delightful Musical
Events Presented in Keokuk

Personnel and Program

S. Francisco Ramos

The above program was presented to almost a capacity house last evening at the Grand by the Ramos Spanish orchestra, which formed the third number in the splendid YMCA entertainment course that is being presented this season for the patronage of the Keokuk people. A more artistic and charming musical entertainment has not been enjoyed here in years. Well delivered, classical and modern compositions gave a variety to the program that was satisfying to every taste. The artistic ear was not offended for the technique and tonal quality of this musical organization was nearly all that could be desired. It is a well balanced orchestra and pours forth a flood of melody. Considering the numerical strength—seven persons—it undertook the interpretation of pretentious compositions, such as the overture from William Tell for instance. An opus of this character demands a large orchestra but the Ramos artists executed the number with marvelous effect considering their limited numbers. The five ladies, clarinetist and cornetist composing the orchestra have achieved large successes in the concert field.

Sr. Regina, in the cornet solo, "Columbia" captivated the audience by his remarkable command of the instrument and was the recipient of an encore, as were the other soloists of the program. They were prodigal in responses to encores.

Ramos, the orchestra leader, [is] an artist on the clarinet, from which he drew unexpected musical effects. He is also an artist as a director, his demeanor exciting no little mirth. His excessive but at times graceful gesticulation was sufficient for the handling of a battalion mass of musicians. This produced the desired psychic effect on the audience even though the artists on the stage were little concerned in his leadership.

The star feature of the program was the violin solo "Melodias Gitanas," with orchestral accompaniment, by Miss Ruth Bowers, who is a rarely gifted performer on the violin with a marvellous command of that instrument. Her delicate expression beautified tonal effect and admirable technique proclaimed her for the real artist that she is. In response to one of the heartiest encores of the evening she gave "My Old Kentucky Home" with captivating but entrancing effect.[18]

The performance at Keokuk was almost the last one in which Ramos conducted the orchestra. He continued to have difficulty getting along with members of the orchestra, and when Rohde fined him a day's pay for his behavior, Ramos wrote a letter to Harrison protesting this action. Harrison replied, "I am not interfering in any way with that western business. You are working for the Redpath Bureau and our contract gives the Bureau certain rights which we have no right to interfere with personally."

The Redpath-Slayton Lyceum finally decided to pay Ramos the remainder of his contract but have him leave the orchestra. Antonio Regina became the director, the orchestra added Lillian Kirksmith to play the flute as a replacement for Ramos's clarinet and they changed their name to the Spanish Orchestra. There were a few alterations to the selections for the concert and a new program was produced.

Ruth told her mother about the orchestra's different atmosphere:

Things have gone so lovely for the past week that it has been like a glorious pleasure trip—every minute. Mr. Regina directs and plays his cornet and Miss Kirksmith of Kansas City joined us Monday. She is an artist on the flute, oh just great, and one of the sweetest girls I ever met…

THE REDPATH LYCEUM BUREAU
PRESENTS

The Spanish Orchestra
AND
Mr. Frederic Irving, Soloist

TOUR OF 1909-10

SR. ANTONIO REGINA, Director	Solo Cornet
FREDERIC IRVING	Bass-Baritone
RUTH BOWERS	Solo Violin
EVA ODELL	First Violin
MABEL KELLOGG	Second Violin
LILLIAN KIRKSMITH	Solo Flute
ROSALIE JACOBSOHN	Solo Cello
LILLIAN BROCKWAY	Accompanist and Pianist

PROGRAM

1. March—"Carmen" .... *Bizet*
2. Overture—"William Tell" .... *Rossini*
   Incidental Cello Solo, MISS JACOBSOHN
3. Toreador Song—"Carmen" .... *Bizet*
   MR. IRVING AND ORCHESTRA
4. Columbia—Cornet Solo .... *Liberati*
   MR. REGINA AND ORCHESTRA
5. American Patrol .... *Meacham*

INTERMISSION

6. Selected Solos—(By Request)
   MR. IRVING WITH MISS BROCKWAY AT THE PIANO
7. Concerto—Gypsy Dances .... *Sarraste*
   MISS BOWERS AND ORCHESTRA
8. Hunting Scene—(Descriptive) .... *Bucalossi*
9. LaTraviata—Flute Solo .... *Verdi-Popp*
   MISS KIRKSMITH AND ORCHESTRA
10. Selection from IlTrovatore .... *Verdi*
    Introducing: "Anvil Chorus," "Gypsy Song," Duet from the Third Act, "Cavatina" from First Act, "Miserere".

A 1909–10 program with the company's new name.

Now to the next chapter. Last Friday evening was a very important night for me for Mr. Horner, the Redpath manager of Nebraska, came all the way from Lincoln to Norfolk to hear me play.

The concert was given in a church and went very well and I had a talk with him after the concert…He made me promise I would accept no engagement for next summer until he had made his proposition.

During the first week of March, the orchestra toured through northeastern Nebraska. After a program

A postcard from Ruth to her boyfriend. "Am surely in the wooly West. Am seeing a lot of real cowboys and Indians. Enjoyed the most delightful weather up till yesterday, but alas— winter again. Was glad to receive your letter but am too busy to write so hope you'll write real soon. Three weeks more, then home for me. We are in the cattle country now. Yesterday took a dandy walk across country. Hoping to hear from you soon."

in O'Neill on March 7, they traveled across the northern part of the state, giving performances in Valentine and Gordon. Ruth wrote to her mother on March 8.

> Well, here we are in Valentine. Yesterday we traveled all day, that is from 6:40 till about five in the afternoon. Then we took a train at 10:40 last night and got here at 2 a.m., went to bed and didn't get up till eleven…
>
> Valentine is on the prairie land. I wish you could see it. For miles and miles as level and flat as a table. Way in the distance you can see the hills. It is glorious weather, we just came in from a walk and I did enjoy it so much. Tonight we have a fright of a time. Take a train from here at 1:30 a.m. and ride till 3:00.

On March 10 they performed at Crawford in the northwest part of the state before heading to the Black Hills in South Dakota. In a letter from Belle Fourche on Sunday, March 13, Ruth described the scenic country that she had visited.

Dearest Mother,

My, I could write a book about the delightful trips we have taken the past weeks and really words can't describe the beauty of these Black Hills.

Thursday we were at Crawford, Neb., one of the most up to date towns we have been to yet. It is situated in a valley surrounded by the most beautiful cliffs and brightly colored hills—one cliff called "Lover's Leap" is over 1000 feet high. We reached Crawford at 8:30 in the morning and stayed at a private boarding house, beautiful place, hard wood floors, etc. and where the dandiest meals were served. In the afternoon we took an automobile ride to Fort Robinson, the army post about three miles from Crawford. The day was glorious and oh we enjoyed the drive thru the winding hills. The army post is quite a large affair, consists of eight companies of 65 to a company and all the officers. The officers' homes are beautiful and the fort is like a city with a post office, gym, opera house, hospital, etc. The guard house was quite a large building and it looked funny to see the sentinels walking up and down in front of the building. We saw one company (cavalry) practicing and oh, such beautiful horses.

On Friday came the most glorious day I have ever spent. We took the train at 7:45 from Crawford, Neb. to Deadwood South Dakota on the Burlington RR. Took breakfast on the diner, sat in a chair car and was real sporty. I'll never forget that ride as long as I live. The RR winds around thru the Black Hills and every minute you can see the most gorgeous sights. The rocks stand out so prominent and form beautiful castle-like shapes. Some are covered with evergreens and others have creeks and waterfalls coming down the sides which are covered with moss. The air is so clear (just think one town where we stopped was 6200 ft above sea level). We could see for miles. We got to Deadwood at one o'clock and had dinner. Another thing I forgot to tell was about some of the hills we climbed. The curves were so sharp that we could see the engine of our train swooping around a curve and here we were nearly opposite it and so near the edge it actually made me dizzy to look down.

At Deadwood we saw the gold mines altho' we didn't have much time to watch them (tomorrow at Lead we are to be guests at a mammoth gold mine, won't that be interesting), and at two o'clock came the most unique ride in a real stage coach for 16 miles, up hill and down vale. At one point we were 5100 ft. above sea level and we saw a point 85 miles distant in South Dakota. At another point we could see off in Wyoming. Talk about your scenery, those distant snow-capped hills on all sides and we went thru some level land where we saw a herd of over five hundred sheep and saw the herder's home. They are built on wheels and look like a gypsy van. We reached Spearfish at 4 o'clock and had our pictures taken…

At Spearfish we played at a beautiful opera house under the auspices of a girls' school. We met a number of lovely girls, after the concert a number came to our dressing room and one slipped a note in my hand telling how much they enjoyed the concert etc.

The note read:

There is a crowd of girls in your audience who are your ardent ad-mirers…We are D.O.D., in other words, the dear old dormitory girls, and we wish you to accept our thanks for a pleasant eve-ning and hope we can hear you play again. The memory of your beautiful interpretations will brighten many dormitory day and midnight spreads. With best wishes of your admirers and hopes for your future fame.

The *Queen City Mail* in Spearfish mentioned Ruth's violin playing: "Sarasate's Gipsy Dances for violin solo were exquisite. Miss Bowers played with fine technique, and put her whole soul into her playing. Her harmonics were beautiful and the one number was well worth the price of admission."[19]

On March 16 the orchestra played at Newcastle, their only perfor-mance in Wyoming. The *News Journal* pronounced the orchestra to be "the finest musical entertainment ever heard in Newcastle…We hope they will come again, and when they do there will be no vacant chair in the opera house. Music like that rendered by this company of artists has an uplifting influence more potent than words read or spoken."[20] Then they returned to Nebraska for the remainder of the month.

After the departure of Ramos, the orchestra enjoyed their final weeks together. Harrison asked Irving for his opinion of the orchestra's perfor-mance under Regina's direction. He wrote:

Mr. Regina directs in a quiet simple musical manner that does not detract nor draw attention away from the music or the rest of the orchestra. The orchestra seems to have given fully as much satisfaction and has received as much commendation under Sr. Regina's direction as at any time during the entire season.

TOP: This is the picture taken at the end of their stagecoach ride. In another letter to her mother, Ruth wrote: "How do you like the looks of the Spanish Orchestra as they landed in Spearfish? Lillian Kirksmith has the reins. Lillian Brockway is beside her. Mabel Kellogg is in the 1st seat, Rosalie Jacobsohn, the 2nd, Eva Odell, the 3rd. Mr. Regina is standing in the rear, while Mr. Irving is the holdup. The funniest old driver, he just matched the rest of his up to date express." On the roof of the large building is a sign for Walk's Blacksmith Shop, a business in Spearfish operated by Martin Walk and his son, John.

LEFT: The Black Hills of South Dakota. Ruth wrote to Gibby: "Oh! This most glorious country, the most magnificent sight. If ever you go west be sure and go from Crawford, Neb. to Deadwood, S.D on the Burlington R.R. Words can't describe the beauty of these hills and rocks."

This photograph shows the costumes and instruments of the members of the Spanish Or-
chestra. Back row: Ruth Bowers, violinist, and Frederic Irving, singer. Centre row (L to R):
Rosalie Jacobsohn, cellist; Antonio Regina, cornetist and director; Mabel Kellogg, violinist.
Front row (L to R): Lillian Kirksmith, flutist, holding instead a clarinet, the instrument Señor
Ramos played; Eva Odell, violinist; and Lillian Brockway, pianist, holding sheet music.

We have not been asked once to make any reduction from price on account of any changes.

The members had a program at North Platte on March 19 and spent the weekend there. Ruth wrote to her mother:

Talk about being royally entertained Saturday and Sunday, listen to this. Saturday aft was out driving with a Yale graduate, whom Mr. Irving knew, a dandy young chap. Saturday eve we were given a dinner at the Commercial Club by six gentlemen…Sunday noon we were at dinner, guests of Mr. Resnick & Thompson, Sunday aft out driving with Mr. Thompson, Sunday eve at dinner with Mr. MacDonnell, and last night we all went to the Episcopal Church and afterwards to the drug store for soda. I never met so many nice men at one time in my life. They couldn't do more for us and certainly made our stay in N. Platte a pleasant one.

At Grand Island Ruth sent a postcard to Charles from the Omaha & Ogden Railroad Post Office: "Rec'd your letter but doubt if I'll find time to write till I get home. We are celebrating our last week by having a glorious time. Best wishes for a happy Easter."

One of the orchestra's programs during the final week was at Ord. Horace M. Davis, publisher of the town's newspaper, was also a press agent for Redpath Chautauqua. He reported on the visit of the Spanish Orchestra and additionally chastised members of the community for not providing a better turnout.

A small audience, altogether too small an audience attended the Spanish Orchestra concert at the Bohemian Hall last Tuesday evening under the auspices of Lodge Dennice. Of course it was during the closing days of the Lenten season and many who otherwise would have attended did not feel like going, but there were not as many Protestants out as might reasonably be expected. It is a sad travesty on the discriminating intelligence of the community that so rare a treat as the program offered Thursday evening was allowed to lose the promoters a considerable sum of money.

Without an exception the music lovers who heard the Orchestra are enthusiastic in their praise of the rendition of the numbers, both the solos and the ensemble work. Miss Bowers, with her violin solos was particularly pleasing and demonstrated a deftness of technique rarely seen in a lady. Miss Kirksmith

OPPOSITE PAGE: The Spanish Orchestra in Nebraska.

with her flute solo was received with an ovation as she stepped to the front of the stage. It will be interesting to learn that on account of the serious illness of the former director, Senor Ramos, the orchestra was reorganized a few weeks ago and that Miss Kirksmith became a member, playing with the flute the parts that had formerly been taken by Director Ramos with the clarionet. To go further in the matter of Miss Kirksmith's connection with the Spanish Orchestra it may be said that soon after the appearance of the Kirksmiths here last fall Miss Gertrude contracted diphtheria and was very sick …

But certainly the most pleasing feature of the concert was the wonderful singing of Frederic Irving. No such voice was ever heard in Ord before and may never be again. The opera house was not large enough to hold it yet the tones were never harsh and the volume of sound did not detract from the sweetness.[21]

The final program of the season was in Columbus at the North Theater. (Constructed in 1902 as an opera house, it still exists as a commercial building.) Ironically, the program was sponsored by the Spanish-American war veterans. According to the *Nebraska Telegram*:

The Spanish orchestra, appearing under auspices of the Spanish war veterans, delightfully entertained a large audience at North [Theater] last Sunday night [March 27]. The veterans will not say just how much money they made, but admit that it was enough to meet the loss they sustained at a prior entertainment and give them a slight boost on the state convention fund which they are trying to raise. The programme was a choice selection of operatic favorites long since listed with the classic in music, with a few selections from among the modern favorites. Among the players was Miss Lillian Kirksmith, who has participated in two Chautauqua programmes in Columbus. Her flute solos and her ensemble playing were much appreciated, and received due recognition. While in the city Miss Kirksmith was a guest at the O.T. Roen house. Miss Ruth Bowers, solo violin, played in manner to win much praise, and in Columbus, which is the home of violinists of merit, she may count her reception complimentary indeed. Mr. Frederick Irving, baritone, appeared in three delightful numbers. Mr. Irving was formerly a metropolitan newspaper man, and since abandoning that profession has been associated with noted operatic stars of the country. The company closed its season with the Columbus engagement.[22]

Antonio Regina wrote to Harrison: "We finished our season last Sunday evening at Columbus, Nebraska, and I am satisfied that everything was alright for the last four weeks. Sorry I could not come to see you as I had to go to reach the Ferullo Band in Kansas City."

Ruth played in more than sixty concerts in five states during her tour with the Spanish Orchestra. She performed with talented musicians in front of large enthusiastic audiences, traveled extensively, and saw a new part of the United States. Through the almost daily concerts her violin playing improved and she gained confidence in her ability as a musician. Most important, Ruth, and the other ladies in the orchestra learned how to perform well musically under difficult circumstances and to assert their rights against the demands of the difficult director, Señor Franasco Ramos.

ELMA B. SMITH

▬▭▬▭▬

AND HER COMPANY

Exclusive Management
SLAYTON LYCEUM BUREAU
Steinway Hall
Chicago.

ELMA B. SMITH COMPANY
MAY – OCTOBER 1910

From Columbus, Nebraska, Ruth traveled to Chicago and then back to Erie. The Erie newspapers had reported on her tour a few times during the winter and one of them enthusiastically described her return and her musical success with the Spanish Orchestra:

> On Thursday a modest, bright and dignified girl stepped from the western train at the old station of Erie, glad to greet the friends that awaited her and to set foot again in the dear home town after an absence of twelve weeks. The girl was Miss Ruth Bowers, the brilliantly gifted young violinist, and the twelve weeks of absence were weeks on tour in concert work where honors and praise came so fast that the time seemed all too short to hold them.
>
> Every time the young artist drew her bow across the strings she seemed to win new appreciation. Everywhere she played to crowded houses, and the audiences wanted to hear her again. Miss Bowers' well-deserved press notices fill a large volume and serve as a pleasing reminder of her very successful trip. In nearly every one is made special mention of the quality in her playing that startles each one of her hearers — the rich breadth and wealth of tone which is so rarely heard, in these days.
>
> Miss Bowers has signed a contract for a twenty weeks' tour in the middle west, under the direction of Alonzo Wilson, of Chicago. It will open May 17th, and will include the Chautauquas of that section. [23]

Ruth had previously played with Elma Smith and her company for a short time when they toured the eastern US. Now she was going to join Elma for her first chautauqua circuit, the Lincoln Chautauqua in Illinois.

Elma B. Smith, the headliner of her company, had been a performer

OPPOSITE PAGE: An official photograph of Elma B. Smith who toured with the Slayton Lyceum Bureau for many years. Redpath Chautauqua Collection, University of Iowa.

ELMA B. SMITH COMPANY

ELMA B. SMITH

Bird Warbler—Monologist—Child Impersonator
—Best of Her Kind in the Nation—
With Violinist and Pianist

To Chautauqua patrons in the sixty Illinois cities where she appeared last year, Miss Smith will need no introduction or commendation.

All admit that she is without an equal in her line of work anywhere in the United States. Thousands have laughed and cried alternately while she was on the platform. Newspapers in some of the largest cities in the state—those conservative papers—have pronounced her the BEST ever heard there.

Her triumph of last season, and the many requests for her return made her the most popular of all the talent. Words cannot do justice to the work of Miss Smith. Hear her and be convinced.

If the prohibition of slavery is good for the black man the prohibition of the liquor traffic is equally good and constitutional for the white man.—Abraham Lincoln, 1853.

11

MISS RUTH BOWERS

OF ERIE, PENNSYLVANIA
Solo Violinist
With Elma B. Smith Co.

Nearly everyone loves really good violin music, the kind which has enabled Miss Bowers to delight thousands all over the Eastern States. Beginning concert work at seven years of age, studying with America's most eminent

teachers, Miss Bowers has truly been called a real artist. Last winter she traveled through the West as the soloist for a well known lyceum orchestra.

MISS AGNES V. AMBROSE
OF BATTLE CREEK, MICHIGAN
Pianist—With Elma B. Smith Co.

A prominent musician once said of Miss Ambrose that she could produce as much music using only one hand as many professionals can with both. Her success in concert work has been remarkable. She has the reputation of never failing to please an audience. Some consider her the best pianist in the Lyceum field.

Whether or not the world would be vastly benefited by a total and final banishment from it of all intoxicating drinks seems to me not now an open question.—Abraham Lincoln, Feb. 22, 1842

12

for many years and appeared on several chautauqua and lyceum circuits. She was known for her ability to impersonate a child's voice and for her bird warbling. Elma was also a monologist, a person who would do a reading that would include the voices of several different characters. Between Elma's selections there would be music. The pianist was Agnes Ambrose, who had toured with Elma for a few years. She would play a couple of solos and was particularly known for her sextet from the opera *Lucia di Lammermoor*, which was arranged to be played only by the left hand. Ruth played a couple of violin solos during the program.

The Lincoln Chautauqua was in its fifth year in 1910. The chautauqua program lasted for six days in each town. There would be an afternoon and evening program that included both music and a lecture. The Elma B. Smith Company was paired with Professor A.A. Hopkins, and both would do two different performances during their day in each town. On the weekend the performers would stay in one town and give a program on both days. Monday was scheduled as a day off.

In early May, Ruth traveled to Chicago, headquarters of the Lincoln Chautauqua. She stayed with the Molls once more and spent time visiting relatives and friends along with attending a vaudeville performance. Before leaving Chicago, she wrote her mother: "Thursday afternoon Mr. Resnik (do you remember the Yale man who entertained the Spaniards at North Platte, Neb., he is here now) called me up and invited me out to dinner and then we went out to Lillian Brockway's and spent the evening."

The next day, Ruth went to see Alonzo Wilson, the president of the Lincoln Chautauqua.

He seemed glad to see me, gave me $5.00 for strings and certainly discouraged me about the next month's trip. Said it was the worst part of the country, southern greasy cooking, no white bread, malaria fever...livestock in the hotel beds and I don't know what all—oh, I think I'll have a grand time!!!

Ruth concluded:

Well, tonight at 8:15 I leave for my barnstorming, take a sleeper and get to Mound City in the morning. Think I shall play:

OPPOSITE PAGE TOP: Elma B. Smith. Redpath Chautauqua Collection, University of Iowa.

OPPOSITE PAGE BOTTOM: Ruth Bowers and Agnes Ambrose in the chatauqua brochure. Redpath Chautauqua Collection, University of Iowa.

1. Hungarian, encore Humoresque
2. Canzonetta/Abendlied, encore Cavatina or Ole Bull

I do hope things won't be as bad as they seem, but I suppose I'll about starve for everybody tells me what I must not eat.

For the Elma B. Smith Company, the 1910 Lincoln Chautauqua started on May 17 at Mound City in southern Illinois. The following day they played at Eldorado, where the local newspaper described the company's program:

> Wednesday the exercises were even more interesting than the day before. Elma B. Smith sustained her reputation as an impersonator beyond all cavil. As a child impersonator we do not think her equal exists and those who heard her impersonate a crying child almost imagined that they were actually in the presence of one and that Elma Smith was only playing on their credulity. Miss Ambrose, on the piano, took the big audience by storm by her performance, and seldom are Eldorado audiences permitted to listen to such music or witness such wonderful performing. The acme of praise is due Miss Ruth Bowers for her wonderful performance on the violin and language fails to convey to the reader the exquisite pleasure of those who listened to her playing. From the low, rich tone to the highest, the audience sat, you might say, captivated. Such gifts are to few mortals given and no doubt Miss Bowers' wonderful powers will do great good.[24]

The Elma B. Smith Company spent the first month traveling around southern Illinois. Usually they only had a short train ride to their next destination. Ruth spent her first weekend at Metropolis, where she wrote her mother.

> Miss Smith was invited out for supper this eve, Agnes is crying in her room and Dr. is homesick—and as for me, oh, we are a swell feeling crowd I can tell you…
> As I told you Mr. [Alonzo] Wilson was here yesterday aft and left at 5:10. The program went very nice and we had a big crowd. This aft I played Holy City and the Lost Chord, yesterday in the aft Hungarian Rhapsody, Kentucky Home, Raff's Cavatina, Abendlied; in the eve Elfentanz, Traumerei, Lost Chord, Kentucky Home. Tonight I'm going to play Adoration, Hungarian

PROF. A. A. HOPKINS

OF NEW YORK

Lecturer — Author — Poet — Editor — Thousands Have Heard Him Speak and Have Read His Books — Meet Him Now Face to Face

Few men living today have had as wide an acquaintance with lecturers, st. esmen, editors and leaders all over the nation as has Prof. Hopkins. An experience of more than twenty-five years on the platform has made him hosts of friends and admirers.

His popular bo..s have been read all over the world. Scholarly, sympathetic, statesmanlike, he has won praise on every hand.

No one can render a poem as well as the author himself. Prof. Hopkins' original poetry, coming from his own lips, will add much interest to the program.

SUBJECTS
Ideas and Men
Rhyme and Reason on the Road
Platform People
Our Schoolmaster
The Cost of a Boy
Barabbas

The liquor traffic is a cancer in society, eating out its vitals and threatening destruction, and all attempts to regulate it will not only prove abortive but aggravate the evil.
10   —Abrahám Lincoln, 1853

Professor Hopkins in the chautauqua brochure. Redpath Chautauqua Collection, University of Iowa.

Rhapsody or else Traumerei, Ole Bull. The leading musician of the burg has requested me to play those.

This is a real nice hotel, the meals are fine (I really saw bread for the first time today) the vegetables are very good and everything so nice and fresh. There is a big magnolia tree in bloom out in front of the hotel, the first I have ever seen. It is so pretty and the roses, oh!, they are grand—bigger than peonies and very fragrant. This town is on the Ohio River...

Well, I better go upstairs and see how Agnes is getting along.

Ruth wrote to her mother from Nashville, Illinois, on May 26. She began by summarizing their activities.

Well, here we are in a decent town again. Since Sunday night we had had lovely weather, which in this work is a very important item. Monday we had a long ride from Metropolis to Pinckneyville—92 miles, and the worst hotel—oh, awful, but we stayed outdoors most of the time so it didn't matter. Mon. eve went to bed real early and Tues. morn practiced a little, took a long walk, and in the eve (5:30) Miss A., Miss S., and I took a drive into the country for an hour. It was pretty and we did enjoy it so much.

Wed. we had only a couple of hours ride and were entertained at a private house. Last eve Mr. Simpson, the Supt. and Mr. Abbott, the assistant and Agnes & myself took a walk to a lake that is just outside of Coulterville. We were going boating but could find no boat.

As a traveling musician, Ruth not only had to perform in the present but also plan for the future. She was only on her second tour and needed to continue developing her reputation so she could secure more engagements. During her time with the Ramos Spanish Orchestra, Ruth had met Keith Vawter and Charles Horner, two of the leading men in the lyceum and chautauqua fields, and both expressed their interest in having her play on future tours. Elma Smith wanted Ruth to be on her upcoming fall and winter tours and she began discussing this possibility soon after the Lincoln Chautauqua tour started. In her letter from Nashville, Ruth wrote:

And now some business. Miss S must know whether I'm going with her this winter and we have been talking about it this morn. She knows I'm worth far more, but she says she can't pay over $25.00 [per week] and all expenses…

The work appeals to me very much and I'm inclined to accept. As I told you in my last letter we wouldn't start till Nov. 14th. The Co. will be all starred alike and I will be advertised all over. We will have seven weeks in Oklahoma, four weeks at Philadelphia and she doesn't know just how many at Seattle, Washington so I would go to the Coast…

She will furnish all cuts and window cards which are very expensive when you get so many. Then too, I like her so much and also Miss A. Of course there is the other side and the salary seems very small.

In a letter from Mount Carmel, Ruth told her mother about being hosted by local people while the Elma B. Smith Company was in Albion.

After the afternoon assembly we were taken on a 2 hr auto trip with the chairman of the committee, Dr. Moss, they are very wealthy, their home is a mansion, and we were surely royally entertained. After the eve program Mrs. Strom gave a little lunch for us at their big home, so you see we were regular society birds.

Ruth mentioned her health: "I forgot to say that people tho't I was getting the malaria so I was marched to the doctors, but altho he gave me some 'preventative medicine' and some cold dope I kept on taking quinine and am feeling fine today." She also informed her mother that she had decided to go with Elma for the fall and winter.

From Alton, where the company gave a program on June 15, Ruth sent a postcard to her mother describing some of their activities while in the town: "Had a very pleasant time here. Were guests at the Baptist minister's home. Went through the largest glass blowers in the world and saw them make bottles." The *Alton Daily Telegraph* discussed Professor Hopkins's evening lecture in detail.

> Professor Hopkins spoke on "The Cost of a Boy." His plea held the large crowd as he pictured an incident in his own life when in conversation with an ex-slave who sold for $2,000. He then compared the cost of a boy until he reaches the age of twenty-one. The estimate is as follows: fifty dollars per year during the first five years, one hundred dollars per year for the next ten years, two hundred dollars a year for the years between fifteen and twenty-one, of that total sum of $2,450.00 cost. The boy will earn on an average during the first twenty-one years, four hundred and fifty dollars. Deducting that amount from $2,450.00 the sum of $2,000.00 remains, the price of a slave in other days.
>
> He concluded that every man was indebted to the world and should meet that debt and become a dividend-paying investment to humanity with his pure life.

The newspaper also reported on the female performers.

> With Prof. Hopkins was the Elma B. Smith Company, consisting of Miss Smith, the queen of Chautauqua entertainers. She caught the ears and hearts of the audience with her first selection, her powers in impersonating are marvelous. Her ability to imitate a bird's voice is a rare gift.
>
> Miss Ruth Bowers the solo violinist delighted her hearers with her skill on the violin.
>
> Miss Agnes Ambrose, pianist, well sustained her reputation as an artist.[25]

The next day, the Elma B. Smith Company performed at Taylorville. This was the first year that the town had a chautauqua program and the *Taylorville Daily Breeze* provided extensive coverage of the event. On June 13, the newspaper reported:

> Taylorville's first Chautauqua will open tomorrow afternoon at three o'clock in a mammoth tent, which will be erected tonight on the west side of the West School grounds. The tent and a man sent out by the Lincoln Chautauqua association will arrive at 6:31 this evening over the B. and O. [Railroad] and a large force of men will be in waiting at the school grounds to help put it in place.

After it was set up, a reporter for the *Daily Breeze* wrote, "The tent is cool, being in a well-shaded place, and the seats are comfortable. The tent has a seating capacity of 800."

The opening afternoon did not go as scheduled.

> The Chautauqua opened yesterday afternoon with Dr. Sea-sholes, the Caveney Co., and a drenching rain! The audience was large and enthusiastic and when the storm and darkness compelled a break in the program, they sang old familiar songs and had a rousing good time. Mr. Caveney proved to be an entertaining speaker as well as clever with the chalk. Mrs. Caveney sang a number of songs and after the storm Dr. Sea-sholes, an able and brilliant speaker, gave his lecture.

The newspaper also reminded its readers to support the chautauqua program.

> If you haven't bought a ticket for the Chautauqua buy one now and prove to the public that you want to be on the band wagon and help boost for a larger Chautauqua next year. Remember, those who chose the numbers for this course had to select talent that could please many tastes. What you especially admire may not please your neighbor, but it's all good and if you believe in your town having a Chautauqua grounds and a yearly assem-bly equal to anything in the state, don't criticise, but get behind and boost.

The Elma B. Smith Company made its appearance on the third day of the chautauqua at Taylorville. The *Daily Breeze* reported:

> A large extension making room for five hundred more people was put on to the tent yesterday in order to accommodate the crowds who came to hear the Elma B. Smith Company and

4 STAR ATTRACTIONS 4

AT THE
Chautauqua Tent To-day

PROF. A. A. HOPKINS
NEW YORK'S
NOTED AUTHOR—LECTURER

Elma B. Smith
AMERICA'S LEADING

Child-
Impersonator
and
Bird Warbler

MISS RUTH BOWERS
Noted Violin Soloist

Miss Agnes V. Ambrose
The Lyceum
PIANIST

Don't Fail to hear these Artists

A poster for Hopkins's lecture and the Elma B. Smith Company's performance.

Looking West on East Market St.
Taylorville, Ill.

Prof. Hopkins. The Smith Company more than made good. Volley upon volley of applause rose in commendation of the fine work of the young ladies.

Ruth sent a postcard from Taylorville to her mother: "Had an immense crowd here of over 800 people last evening. It is a real pretty place. I must have a thin white dress at once—something that won't muss… Either lace, net or some soft material. Will write tomorrow. Love, Ruth."

One of the lecturers on the 1910 Lincoln Chautauqua was George L. Kieffer. In the brochure he was described as "the Gettysburg picture man—Four Years a Guide on the Battlefield—Knows It Like a Book—Two Hundred Fine Views." At Taylorville the Chautauqua committee had a special invitation for Kieffer's program:

> The Chautauqua management both local and general extends a cordial invitation to all the old soldiers, both of the Blue and the Gray, to be guests at the tent on Friday night to hear the "Battle of Gettysburg." The doorkeeper will pass all old soldiers with their wives on that evening, also the widows of old soldiers free of charge. Come to the Chautauqua and we will meet you and treat you nicely.[26]

At the completion of the Taylorville Chautauqua, the *Illinois State Register* wrote:

> Taylorville's attendance is the greatest in any of the twenty-five places the Chautauqua has been held and will in all probability be the record for the season…A permanent committee of five was appointed to take charge of the funds and make arrangements for a Chautauqua next year…The Chautauqua entertainers were well pleased with Taylorville, particularly with the hotel accommodations, which they declared the best of any town they had visited this season.[27]

On Monday, June 20, the Elma B. Smith Company went to Springfield on their day off. In a postcard she sent to Everett, Ruth wrote that she was "watching the others shop…We are going to the parks this afternoon and leave tonight for Sullivan."

The Elma B. Smith Company then traveled to eastern Illinois and began heading north up the state. One of the towns where they performed was Tuscola.

OPPOSITE PAGE: Ruth sent her mother a postcard from Taylorville, Illinois.

Ruth wrote to her mother from there.

At last I have a few minutes to myself so will try and tell you a few things that have happened. In the first place the weather has been scorching and we have had one of the hardest week's jumps of the whole trip, so you can imagine how we have hustled.

From Potomac to Hoopeston we took a 17 mile drive with the worst team of horses I ever saw, were afraid they would drop with the heat and we surely were tired out when we arrived at 1 o'clock after three hours in the dust and heat. Yesterday we got here at 1:50 and kept on rushing. I'm all in, had an awful nervous spell Friday eve and Sat (last night) had such a tremble on the stage I could hardly hold my bow let alone play but I hope to be all right as soon as this heat lets up and I get some rest...

Fri. eve we stayed at a regular mansion, my such swellness (how we wished we hadn't had to hustle away so soon) and were taken to and from the assemblies in one of their big machines and also for a little drive so we could see some of the handsome homes. Hoopeston is a very aristocratic place...Hon. Alonzo [Wilson] appeared on the scenes and gave a "spooch."

Last eve we had another auto ride around the place. I never saw such prosperous country in my life and everybody seems to have money.

If it wasn't for our little drives which cool us off some, I'm afraid we could not stand it.

Ruth also discussed the trip that her mother planned to take to Chicago in early August when the Elma B. Smith Company had several venues in the area.

On Monday, July 4, the Elma B. Smith Company was close enough to Chicago that Ruth went to the city for the day. A few days later, at Bloomington, the company had a celebration. "Had quite a dinner party here today. Nine of us together, Mr. Wilson [president of the Lincoln Chautauqua] from Chicago with us and as it was Miss Smith's birthday we had a good time."

At El Paso, Illinois, Ruth wrote a long letter to her mother on July 14. By now they were almost halfway through the chautauqua tour. The circuit was twenty weeks long; it did not have the variety of locales of the winter tour, and Ruth was not used to the heat or cold rain that often made conditions difficult for performing. Usually, Ruth was cheerful and optimistic, and this is the only letter or postcard in which she describes feeling depressed.

Dear Mother,

A horrid cold rainy day, wind blowing and everything else disagreeable.

Had quite a time this p.m., got rained out of the tent so proceeded over to the Baptist Church where I very beautifully rendered Traumerei, Cavatina and Old Folks at Home with organ accompaniment.

My spirits are certainly below par today for I feel mighty blue and down-hearted. I am so tired of this grind and am so lonesome I don't know what to do with myself. If I could only get home for a week and have a jolly time with people I know I think I would be all right. I surely envy them going camping and picnics, etc. ...

If it were not for our Monday trips I know I never could stand it and I don't know some days whether I can stand even more after this week or not. Believe me, no more 20 week summer trips for me. The other girls vow the same, never again. A couple of months is alright, but five months is too much.

Three of the Principal Attractions at Tuscola Lincoln Chautauqua.

DR. CHAS. L. SEASHOLES.
Thursday, June 23.

PROF. A. A. HOPKINS
Sat. and Sun., June 25-26

MISS RUTH BOWERS

Ruth was billing alongside famed lecturers Charles Seasholes and A.A. Hopkins.

Well, to talk of something pleasant. We girls had a lovely time at Springfield on Monday. We were guests of Mr. and Mrs. Noblett, very wealthy people there and their house guest—Rachel Brenerman, a dandy girl from Bloomington. We got there at 8:30 in the morning, had breakfast and fooled around until about ten when we took a carriage drive downtown. Had lunch and an auto trip to the parks. Oh!, they were so pretty and we were enjoying the beauties of them so much when up came a storm so we hustled for home. It cleared up after a while, so we went down to Mr. Noblett's business—he has an immense laundry and also a dry cleaning establishment. It was interesting to see all the modern ways of washing and I enjoyed going thru very much.

After dinner Leroy, the son, a handsome fellow of 28, took us out in his machine. We were going at 40 miles an hour when whiz

A view of the chautauqua stage at La Moille, Illinois, on July 30. A pennant for Carthage College is visible on the back wall. Elma B. Smith is standing, with Professor A.A. Hopkins seated to her right. Ruth Bowers with her violin is second from right and Agnes Ambrose is seated by the piano. The person on the left is unknown.

went an air brake and I tell you we were frightened for a minute. Of course that put us out of business, so we came back to the house, dressed (in my pink) and proceeded to Mrs. Bliss's home where she entertained for us at a very swell affair. Twenty-two were there, also newspaper reporters, etc. and we surely felt like aristocrats. Met some very pleasant young people, but as usual it was hello and goodbye for we left at six Tues. morning ...

Yesterday we had another excitement. Mr. Clark, a blind man who is a graduate of Chicago University and a very brilliant fellow of 25 years, he is quite rich and has his companion or valet Mr. Moon with him all the time but I never saw anything like it. He gets in and out of his auto like anybody, helps the ladies in and tells them how pleased he is to see them—but that's ahead of my story. He is a friend of Miss Smith, so yesterday at Fairbury he took us for a ride after the aft assembly (Mr. Moon runs his 7 passenger Studebaker) and when we were twenty miles from town bang went a tire. Well, after getting that fixed and proceeding on our way again we hadn't gone over ten miles when bang went another. Oh! They make an awful explosion and every time one breaks it means over $6.00. That one took longer than the other to fix so we just flew into town and just got in the dining room as the door closed for supper, so we rushed thru our meal and hurried to the tent at 7:30 ...

Well, I've written quite a book, so will close as supper is ready.

On their Monday off in mid-July, Ruth and the other company members took a trip on the excursion steamer *David Swain*. From Sparland she sent a postcard to Gibby: "My first river trip and I enjoyed it immensely. The day was glorious and we went from Peoria to Henry, a four hour ride down the Illinois River in this boat."

By late July the company was performing in the Chicago area. The *Naperville Clarion* praised the chautauqua program in their town:

The Lincoln Temperance Chautauqua for the second time, within four years, held its week of education and entertainment in Naperville from July 26–31. To one who has attended every session, and partook of all the good things set before him, finds he cannot discriminate, as to the merits, for every session has been excellent food for the heart and brain.

The mammoth tent occupied the northwest corner of our city park, where the many trees shaded it in the afternoon. It was filled with chairs and comfortable benches with backs to them, and seated about 700 people. At the north end was the speakers' platform, decorated with flags, banners and streamers...To the right of the stage was a small ante-room, for the comfort of the participants. The weather was fine, a trifle warm, perhaps, but there usually was a good breeze sweeping through the tent, and the exercises were of such an interesting nature that bodily discomforts were forgotten.

The *Clarion's* reporter described the Elma B. Smith Company:

Elma B. Smith as bird warbler and child impersonator, was certainly the best ever heard in our city. She has a pleasing voice and manner, her readings were not too lengthy, and she herself was lost in the character she represented. We heard the song of the robin, jay, canary and lark, and the hoot of the owl and the cry of a dog.

She imitated to perfection the wailing of an infant, and the innocent prattle of a three year old child. Miss Smith was greeted with great applause at every appearance.

Miss Agnes Ambrose proved herself a very skillful pianist. And what shall we say of the violinist, Miss Ruth Bowers. She loves her violin and as her cheek lay caressingly against the musical instrument, she fairly made it speak through her soul. She seems at ease as she handles the bow, and her music was highly appreciated.[28]

They finished July with programs at Newark, Plainfield, Waterman and La Moille.

Cora came from Erie to spend the first week of August with Ruth. On Monday, August 8, they went to St. Joseph, along Lake Michigan. Ruth sent a postcard to Everett: "Mama & I have enjoyed a lake trip here today. Back on the job for me tomorrow."

August 15 was the only Monday when the Elma B. Smith Company performed. Ruth sent a postcard to her mother that day. "Am at the Rockford Chautauqua listening to Dr. Hopkins. A busy day, I can tell you. Had a pleasant time while at Belvidere." The following morning she sent a postcard to Charles: "I'm sitting all by myself looking up the river. It is a real hazy morning and everything is so still. You can almost hear yourself think. Played here last night and had a real nice time during the day."

The next stop was at Galena. Ruth sent a postcard to her mother. "Am writing this at [President] Grant's home. Oh, such a hot day! The view is very pretty as the house is way up on a hill." Ruth also sent a postcard to Charles describing Galena: "One of the oldest towns in Illinois and

North Western College Campus, Naperville, Ill.

PROGRAMME (OUTLINE)

TUESDAY	WEDNESDAY	THURSDAY
DR. CHARLES L. SEASHOLES	JAMES HOFFMAN BATTEN	PROF. A. A. HOPKINS
CAVENY COMPANY	NEAL DOW TRIO	ELMA B. SMITH COMPANY
	FRIDAY	SATURDAY and SUNDAY
Full daily programs	BELLE KEARNEY	JOSHUA H. BERKEY
will be issued later	BROWN COMPANY	ROBLEY QUARTETTE
	GEO. L. KIEFFER	

TOP: Ruth sent this postcard to Charles. "Where we are today. Have been busy the past week. Oh! This hot weather—it's been fierce. Be good."

BOTTOM: After Chicago, the company played in Plainfield, Illinois. This was the schedule for the chautauqua program at that town.

TOP: Ruth sent a postcard to Charles from Plainfield. "Back view of the theater where the assembly is held here. It is a beautiful park—boating, bathing, dancing and every other amusement. Over 300 campers are on the grounds."

BOTTOM: Ruth sent postcards to her mother and Charles from Galena.

the home of U.S. Grant at whose home we were this aft—What a pretty place it is and a nice view of the hills."

The *Galena Daily Gazette* reported on both the afternoon and evening programs of the Elma B. Smith Company, which occurred on the opening day:

> The Chautauqua assembly was opened to the public this afternoon when the first entertainment on the week's program was given. Quite a large audience attended and the entertainment was pronounced excellent.
>
> Miss Elma B. Smith, child impersonator and bird warbler kept the audience in an uproar with her clever work. Her impersonations of children were especially clever and highly pleasing to the audience ...
>
> Miss Ruth Bowers, the noted violin soloist showed great skill for technical work and tone and her efforts were highly praised by those who heard her.
>
> Miss Agnes V. Ambrose, the pianist, showed great technical work and won loud applause from the audience.

For the evening performance the newspaper reported:

> Long before the opening an immense crowd of humanity wended their way to the Chautauqua grounds on the east side last evening, and that they were well repaid for their efforts was re-echoed by the tumultuous applause that was accorded the various numbers on the program.
>
> Today it was decided by the management to install more chairs to accommodate the crowd.
>
> The program last evening was highly appreciated, especially the work of Miss Elma B. Smith who was repeatedly encored. In one number Miss Smith depicted the trials of a family going and at a summer resort which made a great hit with the audience. Miss Agnes V. Ambrose at the piano and Miss Ruth Bowers, the violinist, displayed great skill on their respective instruments.[29]

From Galena, in northwestern Illinois, Elma, Ruth and Agnes traveled south through western Illinois for the final month of the 1910 Lincoln Chautauqua.

On September 20, at Kinderhook, Ruth wrote a letter to Charles while she was backstage at the chautauqua performance.

My dear Gibby,

While Dr. [Hopkins] is doing his stunt I shall try and write a few lines to you—provided you approve of the stationery provided here.

Suppose you are home again after your pleasant trip. I thought of you last Wednesday night when the moon was so bright and was wondering whether you boys were enjoying the lake.   ·

Two weeks from today I expect to be home and you can well imagine how anxiously I am awaiting the day till I shall be back to Erie for I expect I shan't be there over five weeks as I'm afraid I shall leave on the tenth of November—will tell you all about my winter tour later when I see you. I am looking forward to a pleasant time this winter for I'm going to travel from coast to coast and hope to see a great deal of the country.

I have surely had some delightful trips and peculiar experiences this summer and altho I have frequently felt lonesome, I am glad that I took the trip for it has been a broad experience for me, which has done me a world of good…Will be in St. Louis next Monday and besides doing some shopping (oh splash) I hope I will have an opportunity to see a good show for I really am quite theatre hungry.

Well, Gibby dear, I must ring off as this is my time for doing a stunt. It won't be very long before I hope to have the pleasure of seeing you and telling you the story of my life. Drop me a line right away for I am always glad to receive your letters. Goodnight, be good, Ruth

From Carrollton she sent a postcard to her mother on September 23: "Have had some great auto rides this week and am waiting now for a machine. The weather is fine, so bright and cool and we are enjoying ourselves but are all studying time tables and counting the days."

The headline for a full-page ad in the Stronghurst Graphic. Lincoln Library.

The cover page for the Lincoln Chautauqua program at Plymouth, Illinois. Redpath Chautauqua Collection, University of Iowa.

On the final Monday of their tour, Ruth went to St. Louis for a day of sightseeing with Emerson Winters, one of the Chautauqua performers. From the train station, she wrote her mother:

Oh! Such a week we have had, for we have all been sick. I think we are all worn out, but never mind, only one week more! The past week so many people have tried to entertain us and make things pleasant but I gave up Sat. morn after getting to Clayton and went to bed. Oh! I never was any sicker in my life. Such pains and vomiting spells. I couldn't get up to play and got worse till they called the doctor. He gave me some dope to warm me up and settle my stomach, which made me feel better in a jiffy. I was at the loveliest home and they just did everything for me so I felt much better yesterday and played at both sessions. Last night Miss Smith gave out and had to be taken home but she feels better today so I think we are all OK again. We all took colds I guess. This awful cold damp weather.

On September 29, Ruth sent a postcard to Charles: "Am getting a lot of pleasure out of my last week. May go home by way of Chicago but if I don't will get to Erie Mon. eve. Be good." The Elma B. Smith Company finished their performances on October 2 in Greenville.

The 1910 Lincoln Chautauqua was Ruth's longest tour, lasting over four months with programs at one hundred communities. The company had been successful, for in their evaluation of the talent for this season the Lincoln Chautauqua personnel rated Elma B. Smith as their top performer, Ruth as their second, and Agnes as their fourth, so the praise the Elma B. Smith Company received in the press was genuine. Ruth's confidence and musical talent continued to develop during the months of playing. Despite her depression in July, she enjoyed performing, traveling, seeing new sights and meeting people. The company was harmonious, something Ruth appreciated after the tour with Señor Ramos. Ruth would be glad to be home for a while and to rest, but she was also looking forward to continuing with Elma and Agnes on their fall lyceum circuit.

The Elma B. Smith Company. Sitting: Elma B. Smith. Standing, L to R: Agnes Ambrose, Ruth Bowers, Bessie Andrus.

ELMA B. SMITH COMPANY
NOVEMBER – DECEMBER 1910

The fall 1910 lyceum program began in mid-November for the Elma B. Smith Company. The company played in Kansas, Oklahoma and Texas, so Ruth had an opportunity to travel to another region of the United States that she had not previously visited. Since the lyceum programs were longer and only one group performed at a venue, Elma added Bessie Andrus, a vocalist, to the company for this tour.

The Elma B. Smith Company met in Chicago and traveled to Kansas City. In a letter to her mother, Ruth noted the large number of Black residents of the city and commented: "Every public place has its signs 'for whites only.' All the trains throughout this part of the country have their 'Negro coaches' and waiting rooms are divided." The tour started with a program in southern Kansas at Cherokee on November 14.

Looking East on 9th Ave., Winfield, Kansas.

A postcard Ruth sent to her mother from Winfield, Kansas. "Had a crowded house and gave a great program. I wish you could have heard it. They have some beautiful buildings for the size and are up to date."

The next day Ruth sent a postcard to Everett from Winfield: "Where we 'show' tonight. If all towns are as good as this no kick coming." She wrote her mother: "The concert was given at the new Methodist Church to over 1,200 enthusiastic people. Every number went off fine. I played Hungarian and Humoresque for an encore, and for a 2nd Zigeunerweisen and Kentucky Home and had to go back and play Lost Chord."

The *Winfield Daily Free Press* described Elma: "tiny, doll-like with a charm of personality and outward appearance, this little bird woman, with her bright eyes and quick movements never loses her attraction." [30]

The *Winfield Daily Chronicle* recounted the program:

BIG CROWD GREETED TINY IMPERSONATOR AND HER COMPANY OF MUSICIANS AT M.E. CHURCH LAST NIGHT

The second number of the Brotherhood lecture course was even a greater success than the first, as far as numbers in attendance go, and that the people were well pleased with the entertainment provided for them was made plain by the repeated encores after every number. Miss Elma B. Smith, child impersonator, was just as charming and fascinating in her unique line of entertainment as on her first appearance here, and this was her third. The large auditorium of the Methodist church was packed to capacity, and standing room, that would command a view of the platform, was at a premium.

The program given by Miss Smith and her company, which includes a pianist, violinist and vocalist, was delightfully diversified, each number being of classical style yet sufficiently popular to meet with the approval of the entire audience.

Miss Bessie Andrus, the charming young vocalist, came second on the program, pleased with her childish naivete and childish manner which at first sight scarcely gave promise of the clear sweet voice, artistically controlled in which she sang her numbers. Miss Ruth Bowers, the violinist, was heartily encored at each appearance, positive proof of her popularity with the audience. Her playing is smooth and musical and shows a masterful knowledge of the violin. [31]

The next day, en route to Kaw City in northern Oklahoma, Ruth sent a postcard to her mother. "I expect we will see some Indians as there is a camp here."

OPPOSITE PAGE: The program for the Elma B. Smith Company's fall 1910 lyceum tour included numbers by vocalist Bessie Andrus, who had joined the company.

Programme

Elma B. Smith, assisted by Miss Ruth Bowers, violinist; Miss Agnes Ambrose, pianist, and Miss Bessie Andrus, vocalist.

Piano Solo—Rhapsodie Hongroise, No. 6...............*Liszt*
MISS AMBROSE.

Vocal Numbers—
   (a) Una voce poco fa'.*From "Barber of Seville," by Rossini*
   (b) My Pretty Jane.........................*Bishop*
MISS ANDRUS.

Violin Solo—Ziguneyweisen ....*Sarasate*
MISS BOWERS.

Readings—Selected.......................*Cooke and Nesbit*
MISS SMITH.

Intermission

Vocal Solo—
   (a) Printemps ....*Stearn*
   (b) Lady Moon ....*Bruhns*

Reading—Story of Patsy...................*Kate Wiggins*

Piano Solo—Sextette from opera "Lucia di Lammermoor"
....*Leschetizky*
(Arranged for the left hand alone.)

Violin Solo—El Fintanz............................*Popper*
Imitations ....
MISS SMITH.

This postcard is from a picture of the Ponca Sun Dance, taken by well-known Kansas photographer George B. Cornish.

While at Kaw City, the members of the company took a ride the following morning, which Ruth described to her mother.

Such experiences! I surely will never forget them. This morning we had one of the most thrilling rides over the vast plains of Oklahoma in an automobile for twelve miles.

I never heard of an auto going over and thru such places as we did; over fields and prairie lands where there was no sign of a road, up hills where by a slip of the wheel we would have gone smashing down a precipice, got lost out in a desolate spot where we couldn't see a house for miles and it was so still, you could almost hear your heart beat. But the climax was when we went right thru a creek in the machine and missed quicksand by a few feet.

Without doubt it was one of the most exciting rides I ever took and we all enjoyed it (now that it's over) for the day is glorious and we were wrapped up so nice and cozy. This is surely a sight passing thru the "wooly west." It is so still that it scares you—not a bird or any noise to break the silence of the miles of plains. We have seen some real Indians in their original clothes, rings in their ears, long braids, bright colored blankets and moccasins. The air is great and I am hungry all the time. So far we

Almeda Hotel, Bartlesville, Okla.

Concert went fine

From Bartlesville, where the Elma B. Smith Company played on November 17, Ruth sent a postcard to her mother: "Where we stayed. This is a fine place of 14,000. They say it is the richest mining (oil) country in the world, it surely looks prosperous and fine new big buildings. Concert went fine."

have lived high. Diner meals nearly every day and the hotels have been good.

Ruth commented on the transportation. "The worst feature with this part of the country are the awful railroads…The trains go bumping and squeaking at about ten miles an hour and consequently while our jumps are not big, it takes us so long to get there, so I don't get much time to do anything but hang on to my car seat."

Their next performance was at Bartlesville, where the local newspaper reported on the program:

ELMA B. SMITH COMPANY WAS GREETED BY A LARGE CROWD

The second number of the Lyceum course, given in the High School auditorium, was witnessed by a large audience which showed its appreciation during the entire program. It was an evening of rare entertainment and the different members of the company were forced to respond to numerous encores.

Miss Smith proved herself a finished artist in her line and her selected readings, being given in the language of babes and children, kept her audience convulsed with laughter. Her second selection entitled "The Story of Patsy" was easily accorded the star piece of the evening. It is the story of a kindergarten teacher's work in the slums of a big city, and is touched with both humor and pathos. The close of the sketch, which ends with the death of the little cripple, Patsy, found many of the audience furtively wiping away the tears of sympathy for the homeless waif.

Miss Ambrose's selections on the piano were well received. The same is also true of Miss Ruth Bowers, violinist, whose work was of a meritorious order. Miss Bessie Andrus, vocalist, is a talented singer and her voice one of rare quality.[32]

Ruth described the evening to her mother.

Oh! You should have seen us at Bartlesville—as I told you we stayed at a very swell place and we certainly were "it." I wore my white dress, evening coat and boa, had a taxi going and a carriage coming home and was presented with a bunch of pink carnations by a friend of Miss Smith—Mr. Holland who was there, a bachelor of 34 who went with us to Collinsville as he had business there. I played Hungarian, Humoresque, Zigeunerweisen, Lost Chord, Home Sweet Home & Old Kentucky. Got two encores on each number and made a big hit.

She noted that she was having trouble with her instrument: "I don't know what I shall do about my bows. They are both worn out and squeaked. We passed a big music store here this eve so maybe I can get one rehaired here tomorrow."

The company next played at Collinsville. Ruth sent a postcard to her mother: "Not much like the immense auditorium at B[artlesville] but then it might be worse. This is just a little burg, a regular western town. Have just finished practicing and am going to take a little walk. It is so warm and pleasant."

When the company arrived at Tulsa on November 21, Ruth sent a postcard of Kendall College to her mother. "Where we do our stunts. The buildings are noticeable for their modern and up to date appearances in this part of the country as everything is new." In a postcard to Charles she said: "A dandy town…The cities are so clean and attractive-looking as everything is new and modern. The country itself is very barren looking and I surely would not care to live in this prairie land." Ruth got her bow fixed while she was in the city and told her mother: "I had my bow rehaired in Tulsa—couldn't use it another day, it got so squeaky, so it is pretty good again although they didn't do any extra good job on it."

The next evening, the Elma B. Smith Company performed at Checotah. The program was at the Tuckabatchee Hall on the second floor of the Sherwood and Avery Building, the hub of Checotah's social activities. The *McIntosh County Democrat* wrote:

> Those who failed to hear the Elma B. Smith Company at Tuckabatchee Hall Tuesday night missed the treat of their life for it was undoubtedly an artistic success...Miss Smith, bird warbler, monologist, and child impersonator, easily captured her hearers by her splendid work. Miss Andrus, vocalist, Miss Bowers, solo violinist, and Miss Ambrose, pianist, were a trio hard to beat, and altogether the Elma B. Smith Company was the best of its kind ever heard in the city.[33]

There were performances at Quinton and at Stroud in the Opera House on November 25. The next day, the company was in Lawton, where the newspaper reported on the Elma B. Smith Company's performance:

> It is sometimes said that a number of women cannot travel together without external quarrels and little "spats." But it can readily be understood that where the company was composed of the four artists who so charmingly entertained a large and enthusiastic audience at the High School auditorium last evening, this would not be the case for the pianist could charm, the singer allayed the passions, the violinist warmed the soul, and the imitator left everyone in a good humor.
>
> The Elma B. Smith Company, as the third number of the High School Lyceum Course appeared last night. A very large audience was present. The pianist, Miss Ambrose, is a finished artist; the vocalist, Miss Andrus, rendered several very beautiful selections and with perfect ease reached the highest notes.
>
> Miss Bowers, the violinist, showed magnificent technique in the rendition of all selections.
>
> As for Miss Smith, "If you can't be a kid and be happy, imitate a kid and make others happy."[34]

After the concert Ruth sent a postcard to her mother: "Where we played tonight [Lawton High School] before a thousand enthusiastic people. Tomorrow we are going out to see a real 'Indian camp' and we are all excited about it. It is so warm that we expect to take a picnic lunch—think of it 28th of November. Everything going fine, having a great time."

On December 2, the company arrived in Texas, performing that evening at Gainesville. Ruth wrote to her mother: "When I get time I am anxious to tell you [about] our entrance to Texas, quite exciting. Have been busy all day, cleaning up and must hurry and get ready. Carriage here at 8, nearly that now. Quite a town. Where we show. [High school, Gainesville, Texas.]"

The Gainesville newspaper described their program:

> Miss Elma B. Smith, monologist and impersonator, assisted by Miss Ruth Bowers, violinist, Miss Bessie Andrus, vocalist, and Miss Agnes Ambrose, pianist, entertained and delighted a large audience in the Tri Mu Club's Lyceum Course at the High School last night. It was an artistic performance of the highest class and was one of the best entertainments ever given here. Miss Smith's impersonations and interpretations were wonderful. Her rendering of Kate Douglas Wiggins' pathetic little story, "Patsy" deserves especial mention. Miss Andrus showed that she had a remarkable voice and her singing of the "Last Rose of Summer" captivated the audience. Miss Ambrose proved herself a pianist and accompanist of marked ability and fairly won the generous applause given her. Miss Bowers gave some beautiful violin selections and made a great hit with the audience.[35]

From Gainesville the company went to Bowie, where they had a program and spent the weekend. Then they traveled to Ringgold, and from there Ruth wrote a letter to her mother. "The people were so nice at Bowie. Yesterday afternoon two young ladies came and took us autoing in their big touring car. We took a big ride and picked some cotton and mistletoe." She expressed concern about her violin: "It doesn't sound a bit good. The strings rattle awfully. I'm afraid it's opening up from being in this dry climate for it certainly doesn't sound good. Sort of scratchy and not a bit sweet. I put on new strings yesterday. I do hope it gets better."

Ruth also noted a change in the weather. "The dreaded norther arrived today. That means a cold, wild north wind that blows terribly and the sand is so thick it just blinds you when you first go outdoors and it is cold out, a great difference from the bright pleasant weather we have had." She was also aware that this was an area where tornadoes occurred. "Every home have their cyclone cellars in their yard where they can run the minute they see the black cloud. They have beds and food down there all ready."

Their next appearance was at Nocona, near Ringgold, where Ruth sent a postcard to her mother. "A glimpse of the metropolis…The joyous part of the occasion was a 14 mile drive over rough country at 5 a.m.—

Hollow Horn Bear, Brule Sioux Chief.
Copyright 1910, Edw Bates.

Following the Sunday excursion, Ruth sent this postcard to her mother: "We see lots of them and are learning to know the different tribes. This tribe wear their hair long." The photograph on this postcard was taken by Edward Bates, a prominent Oklahoma photographer of the early twentieth century.

WEST TEXAS STATE NORMAL, CANYON CITY, TEXAS.
COST $150,000

PAGES 108 and 109 TOP: Panorama of Lone Wolf, Oklahoma. The company played at this town, which was located along the Rock Island Railroad. The Lone Wolf train station is visible in the lower left. Oklahoma, which became a state in 1907, had many small communities like this along the rail lines.

BOTTOM: Busy day, Nocona, Texas.

OPPOSITE PAGE BOTTOM: Ruth sent this postcard to Charles: "Where we did stunts. The building has just been completed. Two weeks from today I will be on my way to Erie. Weather is warm and bright down here."

Pub. by P.N. Oakes.

1170

Santa Fe' Engine - Largest in the World.
110 ft. long — 12 Drive wheels.

Ruth sent a postcard of a large Santa Fe railroad engine and added this comment: "Some engine, don't you think, but even with the big Santa Fe engines the trains thru Texas go awfully slow. Leave Texas on Thursday."

and the coldest morning of the year. We haven't got warmed yet for it was dreadfully cold. My mittens felt good. The cotton is a familiar sight."

On December 10, the company gave a program in Canyon at the West Texas State Normal School, which had just opened in September. The following day, Sunday, the company traveled to Amarillo, where Ruth and Agnes went to church. Before leaving the city on Monday, Ruth did some Christmas shopping.

The Elma B. Smith Company then performed at Canadian, a divisional point on the Santa Fe Railway.

The company's last program in Texas was at Shamrock on December 14. Ruth described the country to her mother. "We are on the plains—just as flat as a table for miles and nothing but a barren burnt-up looking country with nothing to break the monotony except a lonely hut now and then." She noted: "My violin is sounding better these days, I do hope it keeps up."

On December 15, the company returned to Oklahoma and performed at Clinton. They finished the fall tour in southwest Oklahoma with programs almost to Christmas. Among the venues where they played were Lone Wolf, Hollis, El Dorado, Granite and Arapaho. The *Hollis Post Herald* described the Elma B. Smith Company's performance: "The program, which was held at the Methodist Church, was the third of the lyceum series and had a large audience…The violinist

is probably the best a Hollis audience has ever had the pleasure of hearing...The baby tale of Miss Smith is alone worth the price of admission."
The newspaper reminded the residents of Hollis that "the way to have
high kind entertainment is to encourage it with your patronage."[36]

On Christmas Day, Ruth sent a postcard to Charles Gibson from
Wichita, Kansas: "I'm started for home. Hope to reach there before this
does, at about noon Monday. Merry Xmas."

Although this lyceum tour was a short one, it had been successful.
The Elma B. Smith Company played to large crowds and received favorable press reviews. Ruth enjoyed visiting a new part of the United States,
and she was looking forward to even more traveling during the winter
1911 lyceum tour.

ELMA B. SMITH COMPANY
JANUARY – MARCH 1911

After a couple of weeks of holiday, the Elma B. Smith Company started their winter tour in mid-January. This one would have the most traveling, and during the following two months, Ruth would play at cities along the Atlantic Ocean, on the Pacific coast, and in Canada.

The Elma B. Smith Company produced promotional material that described each of the performers and included a photograph. The lyceum bureau that organized the tour would send a copy of this information in advance to newspapers in the towns where the company was scheduled to play. A week or two before their performance, many newspapers published an article about the company and included excerpts from the sheet. In its March 2 edition, the *Pasco Express* (Washington) published a detailed description of the Elma B. Smith Company that was probably copied directly from the promotional sheet:

ELMA B. SMITH COMPANY

Probably no entertainer who has ever come before the American public deserves stardom more than Elma B. Smith. She is unquestionably the greatest imitator of children, birds and animals now before the public. Her imitation of birds, babes and children are a unique feature of her work and are the best of their kind on the platform. Her imitations of children are so real and lifelike that they are the talk of the town for days after her departure. For the seventh consecutive season Elma B. Smith and her excellent company have traveled the United States from coast to coast, and have been pronounced the best popular company traveling.

BESSIE ANDRUS

Miss Andrus has had the advantage of being reared in a musical atmosphere. She has been under the most noted teachers in

OPPOSITE PAGE: The Elma B. Smith Company ready for traveling in the winter. L to R: Ruth Bowers, Agnes Ambrose, Bessie Andrus, Elma B. Smith.

America's musical center, Chicago, and her natural gift, which captured thousands in her childhood when she was hailed as "The Tiny Patti," having developed, today her voice shows the effect of her efficient and artistic musical training. She has been a great Chicago favorite, where she has entertained in scores of wealthy homes. Miss Andrus is a concert favorite everywhere she appears.

MISS RUTH BOWERS

Miss Bowers has appeared in concert work since she was seven years of age, when she gave promise of becoming a great violinist. This promise of early childhood has been fulfilled and today she ranks with the finest violinists on the concert stage. She has studied with eminent teachers including Otto Malms, Henri Ern and Franz Koehler. Her repertoire includes works of great masters and the best modern composers known for the violin. Miss Bowers has a charming stage presence, with an unassuming and pleasing manner; in fact she never fails to please.

MISS AGNES V. AMBROSE

Miss Agnes V. Ambrose, of Battle Creek, Michigan, is a very accomplished pianist. Having studied in various institutions and with famous teachers, she always is able to please her audiences. Miss Ambrose plays with exquisite feeling and with equally great brilliancy. Her playing is musical, with fine technique, and it is that of an artist. By some she is considered the best pianist in the lyceum field. Certainly she is a favorite, and has won an enviable reputation because of the high grade work of the platform and her wonderfully pleasing personality.[37]

During the first part of the winter, the company played at locations in the eastern United States, mainly in Pennsylvania. They started with programs in Kane and Emporium, small towns in northern Pennsylvania. Following the second program Ruth sent a postcard to her mother, telling her, "The weather has been great and the scenery is quite pretty among the hills. The concerts have gone OK and the crowds have been enthusiastic." After a couple of days in the Harrisburg area and a day in Philadelphia, they traveled to Reading, where Ruth described her adventures in a letter to her mother on Sunday, January 22:

Have been so busy sightseeing that I have neglected to write. We arrived at Phila[delphia] Friday morn at eleven, had lunch and went to Keith's Theatre to a very good matinee, left at 6:10 for Summerdale and gave our concert to a medium sized audience there. The program went fine and I was highly complimented but there won't be any notice as it is a small suburb. Yesterday morning we went sightseeing. Went to Wanamakers—it is a glorious store similar to Fields at Chicago. They have an Egyptian Hall there with a mammoth big organ and music room where they give concerts every day. We also went to Independence Hall and saw the historical things. Left there at one thirty for Leesport, a little German town, and gave our "show" in a big barn of a place. Mr. Kieffer [the Gettysburg picture man from the 1910 Lincoln Chautauqua] arrived on the scene at six and Miss Smith is happy. He came on to Reading this morn. And they are out for a walk and I am in my room with the *Saturday Evening Post* [magazine], a box of candy and a bunch of violets and a dozen letters to write …

We have seen a number of beautiful sights this week. On Thur. we had a three hour ride along the Susquehanna River. It was such a pretty day and the river looked so pretty. At one ferry landing we passed there was a big blockade of ice floating down the river and causing a great deal of excitement.

But when we got to our destination!!! The great metropolis of Greene is about a mile from the station, so after having our supper at the hotel our taxi drove up in the form of a big wagon filled with straw and blankets and we—the famous Smith Company—clamored in! It was a beautiful moonlight night and the "buxom girls that kissed the boys" were all there and we passed some foot passengers with lanterns. There were over six hundred in the audience and rigs and horses…a little different from the style we put on the next day at Phila. I had my first ride in a subway on Friday and enjoyed the sensation very much.

We are to be in Phila. almost every day next week so will have an opportunity to see and hear some good things. Just think, I am going to hear Mischa Elman [a famous Russian violinist] at his only performance in Phila. on Wednesday aft. I am so anxious to hear him and never dreamed I would have the opportunity…A week from today I hope to be in N.Y.

Ruth also wrote to Charles: "The first week of trip is over and if the following ones are as pleasant, this will surely be an interesting experience, for I have enjoyed every minute of the past week." After describing her activities for the week, she said: "This surely is a great life and a splendid education, I enjoy it very much and especially being associated with four such congenial girls. We see the funny side of such 'barn storming' performances as we had at Greene so get all the pleasure we can."

The Elma B. Smith Company spent the next week in Philadelphia, traveling from there to their performances. These included two in Delaware, at Georgetown and Bridgeville, along with two in Pennsylvania, at Chatham and Wycombe.

Ruth sent a postcard of the Philadelphia subway to her mother. "My! But the cars go fast. Heard Mischa Elman yesterday and he was great. We are playing at suburbs near here so have been in Philadelphia all week."

The company decided to take a trip to New York during the last weekend of January. Ruth wrote two letters to her mother describing the visit. The first was written from the Prince George Hotel where they stayed:

> We arrived last eve from Phila at seven o'clock and the Penna. Terminal station alone is worth going miles to see. The most mammoth structure of marble I ever saw. It was just opened on Nov. 25th and is the largest station in the world …
>
> Today we slept till ten, had breakfast and at twelve o'clock we journeyed out to see sights. There are no streetcar lines on 5th Avenue and these big machines (like the old horse cars) with their funny little stairway up to the top where seats are arranged like a street car, well situated for seeing everything. Up the stairs we climbed and took a two hour ride. We couldn't have chosen a better time to have gone for people were promenading home from church and such a gorgeous array of dresses and silk hats and canes, poodle dogs, etc. I wish you could have seen it. It gave one an idea of the fabulous amount of wealth there must be here and to see the street crowded with autos and carriages and the famous hotels and residences not to mention the Singer Bldg, Flatiron, etc…Went out Riverside Drive, saw the Hudson McKinley Memorial, Carnegie Music Hall, Metropolitan Opera, and a number of millionaires' homes.
>
> Our other trip was taking the ferry from the harbor out to Government Island and going up into the Statue of Liberty. I had no idea it was so big until I took the long walk up to the entrance and elevator four stories and then the other girls walked up the circular staircase inside the statue while I looked at the Brooklyn Bridge and took in the dandy view from the balcony of the city.

Ruth's second letter told about their last day in New York and some of their programs in New Jersey the following week:

Ruth sent a postcard to her mother: "[This] gives you an idea of how the 5th Ave. looks as the people come from church."

It has been a very enjoyable trip at New York. Monday morning Agnes, Jo and I went on a ride out to Agnes' friend's home on 5th Ave. (an old school chum of hers) and she took us to Central Park where we spent over four hours. It was at the fashionable hour (eleven o'clock) and we saw lots of people on horseback, on the bridal path, autos and carriages; the statues etc. and then we went to the Metropolitan Museum of Art…I'll tell you all about it when I get home. We had lunch at the Art Restaurant and left N.Y. at three forty, getting to Phila at half past five—took the ferry to Camden and we gave our concert at the Centenary Methodist church—it was a big church and we had a fine audience. The program went off great. Agnes had her Steinway grand which always makes her feel good. Last night we were at a little place called Elmer but had a packed house. We didn't get there till about seven o'clock from Phila…This (Bridgeton, NJ) seems to be quite a place and we are in the big opera house. Tomorrow at Trenton we are at the Y.M.C.A.

The *Bridgeton Evening News* recounted the music that Ruth played: "An accomplished violinist, Miss Ruth Bowers was a favorite from the first. She gave *Zigeunerweisen* by Sarasate and for an encore played without accompaniment 'My Old Kentucky Home' with a beautiful as well as unusual duet effect. 'Elfentanz' (Popper) was also warmly applauded and she played an encore that was the crowning selection of all. Her work was artistic in every way."[38]

After a program at Brogueville, the company had a long train ride to Punxsutawney in west central Pennsylvania for a performance on February 4. The lyceum program was sponsored by an unusual organization, the town's Central Fire Company. The *Punxsutawney Spirit* reported that Elma Smith's "child impersonations, warbling and monologue were an evening's entertainment in themselves." The newspaper also commented that Ruth "rendered the works of the great masters with a technique and understanding that made the audience hunger for more."[39] The Elma B. Smith Company finished the eastern portion of the winter tour with a program at Millersburg and one at Gettysburg on February 7. There they visited George Kieffer again, and some of the boys at Gettysburg College arranged a dance for the four ladies following their concert.

Ruth returned to Erie for a few days before continuing on the winter tour. She found that the city was having an epidemic and wrote to Charles: "As always I was very glad to get home again even tho' it is for so short a time. Erie is having a very serious epidemic of typhoid fever, over four hundred cases at present and deaths reported every day. There are over eight thousand people in the city under physician's care, so you may well imagine how much sickness there is here—I think it is a good thing I am leaving so soon, don't you?"

The members of the Elma B. Smith Company reunited in Chicago in mid-February. While she was there, Ruth went to the Redpath office and met Harry Harrison, the manager. She wrote to her mother: "Mr. Harrison was lovely to me—said he received a letter from Vawter about me, said they wouldn't know for about a month whether they would have a good opening for me."

The western tour had barely started when a major change occurred in the Elma B. Smith Company. In a letter to Gibby from Vermillion, South Dakota, on February 24, Ruth explained what had happened:

After the excitement of the past ten days I'll make another attempt to write. I found a letter last eve. to you that I had neglected to mail but hope this one reaches Station A.

Where shall I begin? As you know I left Erie on Tues eve. for Chicago where I played on Wed. eve. Thus. aft. I attended the New York Hippodrome which is having a run at the Auditorium, afterwards went to a Chinese restaurant for dinner and then to Herbert's musical play—*Sweet Sixteen*, which by the way is fine, the music is catchy and tuneful.

The Hippodrome is surely a wonderful spectacular production. There are over 350 people in the cast and the electrical display is gorgeous.

On Friday eve. left Chgo. for southern Illinois where we filled three engagements at Augusta, Quincy, and Litchfield and got back to Chgo. on Wed. In the evening I went to a dance at the Colonial Club and enjoyed it "muchly."

Thur. eve—last eve—left Chgo. and here I am in Vermillion, S. Dak., where we play tonight. The state university is here and altho the place is small, it is really pretty. It is on a high hill and the homes are beautiful. You see, I know, for I've just returned from a walk (are you having such a gorgeous day at Pgh.).

If you please sir, I "the kid" of the Smith Concert Co. am Manageress and altho I've had the position less than 24 hours, I'm ready to give it up. Oh ho! Too much worry and trouble!

While we were in New York last mo. Miss Smith appeared before the Keith Managers with such howling success that they are all clamoring for her. Absolutely I never saw anything like it, the way she "took," so after a week's rest she makes her debut at New York as a vaudeville star the 2nd week in March.

You can imagine the excitement it caused in the Company! Her contract was signed for the three weeks western trip, and altho she tried to cancel it they were anxious for the "Co.," so she obtained a substitute, gave Rufus some instructions, put the "gals" under her capable management and here we are!

If you hear of four girls getting stranded on the Pacific coast please send a relief check at once for absolutely I don't know any more about money affairs than a rabbit—but I'm into it and will have to do the best I can. Wish you were here to help me. We leave Sunday morning for Spokane, Wash. And I'm sure we will enjoy the trip. I'm anxious to see the real west and to cross the Rockies.

Those who have gone by the Chicago, Milwaukee & St. Paul (the Northern Pacific) say it is such a picturesque route so I think we will go that way. Did I tell you we are to play at Vancouver British Columbia, so I will get to have a ride on the Pacific Ocean...

Now Gibby, don't fail to write to me often, for I shall be so glad to receive your letters and I will endeavor to keep you posted as to how the Manageress proceeds with her duties. I forgot to tell you Miss Smith is to be at the Grand soon and you must not fail to go and see her and try and make it pleasant for her for she is the dearest little girl you ever met and I know you will love her as everybody does who knows her...

On the same day, Ruth sent a letter to her mother describing the two people who joined her and Agnes.

Nettie [Elma Smith's sister] is the vocalist of our revised troupe and is so cute all she has to do is just stand up and smile at the audience and she makes a hit. But she has a real sweet voice altho' it isn't very strong. Elma B. Wilson's (isn't it funny her first name and middle are the same) readings remind me of Bess Barton's [a well-known chautauqua and lyceum reader at that time]. Her manner on the stage is like her too. She does some child work which is good but far from what the original Elma's are. But I think our program is very attractive and we will get thru our three weeks OK.

Two days later, Ruth sent a postcard to her mother from St. Paul, Minnesota. "Had great excitement the past 24 hrs but hope we get off for Spokane tonight. Came here from Yankton on the sleeper last night. Taking in sights."

Lewis Street, Looking, West, Pasco, Wash.
Copyrighted 1909 by C. C. Townes.

A view of downtown Pasco. The Northern Pacific Railway bridge across the Columbia River is visible in the center left.

On the trip, Ruth sent a postcard to her mother from Miles City, Montana. "Just to let you know we are on our way. Stopped here a few minutes so I got off. Scenery is gorgeous." In another postcard, sent on March 2, she commented, "Spokane looks like any eastern city—up to date and bustling."

In Washington, the company played at some towns along the Northern Pacific Railway line. The *Lincoln County Times* reported on the program at Davenport, southwest of Spokane:

> The Elma B. Smith Company, the last number of the entertainment course given by the Men's Club, was well attended and the audience was very pleased by a really excellent program. Miss Bowers, the violinist was appreciated very much by the audience and was kind in responding to encore after encore. This number completed the entertainment course of the Men's Club and the courses just about paid for themselves, leaving a small amount to be paid from the treasury.[40]

There was a performance in Pasco, in southern Washington along the Columbia River, on March 6 and one in Prosser the next day. Despite the change in the company and the added responsibilities, Ruth was able to enjoy the tour. She wrote her mother: "The weather is great—we are having a fine time. The burgs are small but have lovely hotel accommodations."

The company reached Seattle on March 11 and the following day she told her mother in a letter: "I'm having such a good time, I wish you could see this country with its beautiful hills and cliffs and everyone seems so prosperous. We were at North Yakima for a few hours yesterday and saw the famous apple orchards. Everything is spring-like and people are sporting summer hats and spring suits."

After two programs in British Columbia, the Elma B. Smith

Ruth sent this postcard to her father: "We saw this Indian relic, the totem pole this morning...I like this place so much. The bay looks like Erie harbor and looks like the peninsula on the other side of the harbor, only much bigger as the ocean steamers all come up to Seattle. Hope to see the ocean tonight on our way to Vancouver."

PERFORMING IN BRITISH COLUMBIA

A postcard Ruth sent to Gibby after a visit to this large park in Vancouver.

Ruth sent a second postcard to her mother: "A sample of the scenery we saw this morning. There is a beautiful park here too...Take a boat for Nanaimo at 2 o'clock." Siwash Rock is a prominent location along the ocean in Stanley Park. In 1911, there was no seawall around the park, and there was very little settlement along the north shore of Burrard Inlet, which can be seen in the background.

The Nanaimo Opera House was a prominent building in the city and the center of cultural events. The top two floors were a hotel. The opera house, on the bottom level, had seating for about eight hundred people as well as an orchestra pit, and it hosted many large productions, including the New York Metropolitan Opera. A-04632, Royal BC Museum and Archives.

The four women traveled on an overnight boat trip from Seattle to Vancouver. The next morning Ruth visited Stanley Park and did some shopping.

The company took a Canadian Pacific Railway steamship to Nanaimo, the second-largest city on Vancouver Island, playing that evening at the Nanaimo Opera House. In an article promoting the program, titled "Society Event Monday Night," the *Nanaimo Free Press* wrote that the Elma B. Smith Company "is heralded as the best musical and humorous company to visit the city this season...The Opera House management are paying a big price to secure these artists for local theatre patrons."[41]

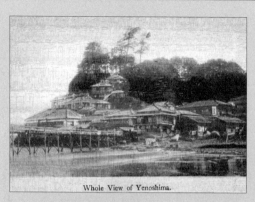

Whole View of Yenoshima.

This is the cover page of the folded rice-paper note that Ruth used for her letter to Gibby.

The company returned to Vancouver the next day and performed that evening at the Central Methodist Church, a large building located at the corner of Dunlevy Avenue and Pender Street in the Strathcona district, a few blocks east of the main part of the city. Ruth and the other women stayed at the Metropole Hotel near the corner of West Cordova and Abbott streets. The next morning, Ruth visited Vancouver's main Japanese district, which was nearby. There she purchased some Japanese rice paper and wrote a letter to Gibby. The cultural experience of visiting a foreign country must have evoked a feeling of patriotism from Ruth:

> Just a line to let you know all is well up in this part of the country. Have had two glorious boat rides and enjoyed the picturesque scenery but I tell you America is good enough for me ...
> The Japanese stores are beautiful and have handsome displays. Their stationery struck me as being so odd—couldn't refrain from sending you this, especially if there is any danger of Elmer seeing it, for I know how he loves fancy paper. Oh ho! [The Gibson family had a small card and wallpaper shop in Pittsburgh. Elmer was Gibby's youngest brother.] Back to the states this afternoon and no more don't cher know Englishmen thank goodness.

Company performed at Burlington and Marysville, Washington, both located on the Great Northern Railway between Vancouver and Seattle. This was the first year that Marysville had a lyceum program. In a front-page article titled "Lyceum Course for Marysville," the *Marysville Globe* wrote on October 14, 1910:

> A lecture and entertainment course will be given this fall and winter under the auspices of some of the leading business and professional men of the city.
> Last spring it was decided to have this course, and complete arrangements were not made until recently.

The purpose of this course is to give the people of Marysville and vicinity high class lectures and entertainments at the lowest prices possible.

The different numbers are of the very best. The talent of this course has been procured from the Pacific Lyceum Bureau of Seattle. Great care has been taken to select a well-balanced course that will be appreciated by all.[42]

The article described the five programs scheduled for Marysville and noted that the Elma B. Smith Company "represents the very best traveling under a lyceum bureau." The newspaper urged the town's citizens to participate. "In getting a season ticket your seats may be reserved for the entire season and at the same time, you will help us to make the course a success."

After the performance in March, the Marysville newspaper reported:

The Elma B. Smith Company gave the last number on the entertainment course and it was considered an excellent program by all who attended. Miss Ruth Bowers is a master on the violin. She was encored time after time and never failed to please everyone. Miss Agnes Ambrose is without question the most accomplished pianist that every came to Marysville. Her execution and technique is wonderful.[43]

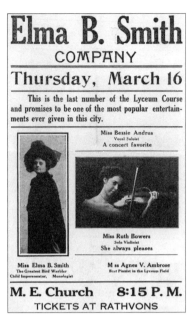

The Elma B. Smith Company was popular everywhere it traveled.

Ruth collected this postcard of the Everett & Seattle plank road near Marysville.

Mt. St. Helens from Spirit Lake.

At Castle Rock, which is not far from Mount St. Helens, Ruth collected this postcard.

The company gave a program at Skykomish on St. Patrick's Day on a Friday evening. Ruth wrote her mother: "They gave a dance after the concert in honor of St. Patrick—oh it was some town I can tell you." There was only one hotel in the town and "the men drank and caroused all night and kept us awake with their yelling…We were thankful to get up at five o'clock and get out." The company's last performance in Washington was at Castle Rock.

As they traveled south through Oregon, the company gave programs at three venues: Cottage Grove, Ashland and Klamath Falls. On the train ride between Ashland and Klamath Falls, Ruth wrote her mother: "We surely had a great time the past three weeks. I have seen the most glorious country and the grandest sights. I'll never forget my trip to the coast." She also told her about a special trip at the end of the tour. "Nettie and I are going to visit the Robleys at Monterey a day or two. [The Robley Quartet was on the 1910 Lincoln Chautauqua.] I received an urgent invite from Bayard's sister, Winifred, and several from the boys, so I think I shall go as I may never be in this part of the country again."

The Klamath Falls newspaper reported:

> An enthusiastic audience and a highly appreciative one listened to a well rendered program at the Houston opera house last night and it is safe to say that the curtain came down too soon for everyone in the audience.
>
> The entertainment is the first of a series to be given by the Pacific Lyceum and that they will be instructive and entertaining

goes without saying after the performance of last night.

Professors Dunbar, Faught and Swan are to be commended for their successful efforts in bringing this talented company — each one of which is a special artist in her line — to Klamath Falls and that Klamath Falls prove appreciative of the effort was fully attested by the applause that accompanied each number and the reception for each performer after their number.

The newspaper also commented that "Ruth Bowers, the violinist, kept the audience spellbound by her music."[44] The next morning, Ruth wrote to her mother. "The four of us are surely happy this morning for we ended our tour in great glory last night at Klamath before a crowded house."

The visit with the Robleys was a special occasion for Ruth, as she wrote to her mother:

Had a fine time at Monterey at the Robley Ranch. The four quartette boys were there, Bayard's brother Spencer, and his two sisters. They were all perfectly lovely to me and I seemed to make quite a hit with them. We had a regular camping party, took long walks up the mountain trails, etc. and on Sat eve Miss Griffin and her brother gave a real country dance for me. (They are Robleys nearest neighbors, a lovely girl about twenty-five.)

Ruth traveled to Los Angeles, where she and Nettie began their return trip on March 28. She sent a postcard to her mother. "Left Los Angeles at 11 Tues. morn and expect to reach Salt Lake today (Wed) at three p.m. We are crossing the plains. Will get to Chicago Sun. eve and leave for Erie by Tues."

The winter tour was an eventful experience for Ruth. She visited New York and Philadelphia for the first time and attended several cultural events there and in Chicago. Despite the difficulties with the western leg, Ruth enjoyed the adventure, particularly all the new places she visited: the Rocky Mountains; the states of Washington, Oregon and California; the Pacific Ocean; and her first trip to Canada. As she was returning, Elma sent Ruth a postcard with an apology and told her: "I shall never forgive myself for starting you out with not sufficient funds." After Ruth wrote her a letter, Elma sent another card: "Your letter is a masterpiece. Shall keep it as long as I can...It was a cure for me...I have felt better since reading it."

"Don't you think our faces are our fortune? The happy Clarke-Bowers Company." (L to R) Ruth Bowers, C. Edward Clarke, Grace Desmond.

CLARKE-BOWERS COMPANY
JUNE – SEPTEMBER 1911

By 1911, there were six chautauqua circuits operating, enabling more lecturers and musicians to perform for the public. It also provided the opportunity for the talent to play on a different circuit each year, increasing the number of people who heard them while giving the audience new performers. This helped to maintain the vitality of the chautauqua circuits. The *Forest City Summit* discussed this concept in an article at the end of the 1911 chautauqua: "While everyone has enjoyed this year's program, yet it would not do to have the same one next year. The past record of Mr. Vawter and his system is sufficient guarantee to make us feel safe in saying that he will spare no efforts to make next year's program as good or even better, if that be possible."

After a year of touring with the Elma B. Smith Company, Ruth wanted to play in a group that included more music in its performances and to be on a different circuit. The experience of managing the Elma B. Smith Company for the western portion of the winter lyceum tour gave her the confidence to take a lead role in forming a new musical group. In late March Keith Vawter signed Ruth to a contract for the 1911 Redpath-Vawter circuit and put her in partnership with C. Edward Clarke, a baritone singer who had been on a chautauqua circuit a few years previously. Together they formed the Clarke-Bowers Company and became one of Vawter's musical groups for that summer.

This was a significant advancement in Ruth's musical career, for Redpath-Vawter was the largest and best known of the chautauqua circuits in the Midwest and western United States at that time. It included towns in Iowa, southern Minnesota and northern Missouri, so there was more traveling than on the Lincoln Chautauqua. Almost all of the towns on Vawter's 1911 circuit had a seven-day program, and the schedule allowed for fewer days off than the Illinois tour. The tents were bigger, the audiences larger, and there were more performers, so the chautauqua was a major event in most of the communities and the performers usually had a large, enthusiastic audience.

C. EDWARD CLARKE

C. Edward Clarke, "the Canadian baritone."

C. Edward Clarke, "the Canadian baritone," graduated from the University of Toronto in 1903 with a degree in music and then went to Europe for further studies. In 1906 and 1907, he was with famed violinist Leanora Jackson on a transcontinental tour of the United States and Canada, and in 1907 and 1908, he headed the Charles Edward Clarke Concert Company, which spent twenty-three weeks touring. Clarke then went to Paris for almost two years, where he studied under the famous singer Jean de Reszke, before returning to the United States in the late summer of 1910. The manager of the Redpath-Slayton wrote on October 1 that Clarke "is greater than ever. He made his first appearance on his return to America, at Winona, at the International Lyceum Association Convention a few weeks ago, and you will be pleased to know that he simply carried everything before him." *The Lyceumite and Talent* magazine noted that "his voice has all of its old time sweetness, greatly increased in range and power and flexibility." Clarke then embarked on both a fall and winter lyceum tour before moving to Chicago and taking a studio in the Fine Arts Building, the premier building for artists and musicians in the city.

OPPOSITE PAGE: "Always remembering our happy touring days and your splendid playing. Lovingly, Grace." Grace sent this picture to Ruth in 1913.

Clarke-Bowers Recital Company

C. Edward Clarke	-	*Baritone*
Ruth Bowers	- -	*Violinist*
Grace Desmond	- -	*Pianist*

Management Redpath-Vawter Chautauqua System

Vocal—Irish Names........... Hilton Turvey

Violin— Zigeunerweisen ....Sarasate

A collection of Gypsy national and folk songs

Piano—À la bien Amie...............Schuett

Vocal—Torreadors Song (Carmen)...... Bizet

Violin—Hungarian Dance.............Hauser

Duet—Violin and Voice

I Live and Love Thee........ Campana

MR. C. EDWARD CLARKE
Pupil of Jean de Reszke of Paris, France
TEACHER OF SINGING
629 Fine Arts Bldg. = = = **Chicago**
Classes Resumed Sept. 18

A program, probably for the afternoon performance, for the Clarke-Bowers Company.

On May 4, Clarke sent a postcard to Ruth: "I saw Vawter a few days ago. We will begin about June 27th or 28th. Our pianist is Miss Grace Desmond, 4430 Vincennes Ave., Chicago, Ill—a good one. If you come thru to Chicago a day or two ahead you can rehearse with her here. Hope to see you in May."

Desmond was a young pianist from Chicago who had studied with two prominent piano teachers in the city, William Sherwood and Fannie Bloomfield Zeisler. In January 1911, she was the pianist for Clarke for a few weeks at the end of his lyceum tour with the Riner sisters. When Katherine Ridgeway, one of the foremost lyceum readers, needed a pianist for two weeks in March 1911, the manager of Redpath-Slayton wrote: "We have just the artist. She was out with Charles Edward Clarke and made big."

The format of the program was similar from town to town. The musical groups performed in the same order in almost every community, with the Clarke-Bowers Company appearing on the third day. They played for about a half hour in the afternoon and forty-five minutes in the evening.

James Francis O'Donnell, a monologist, was the afternoon lecturer at the beginning of the summer, but during the tour they had

---

**THE MUSICAL PERFORMERS OF THE 1911
REDPATH-VAWTER CHAUTAUQUA**

Vawter hired many talented musicians for his 1911 chautauqua circuit. Some of these groups performed for many years and were well known.

A.F. Thaviu's band, which was active from 1905 to 1944, was one of the most prestigious of his time. The 1911 season was the first year that Thaviu played on the chautauqua circuit. Thaviu's band was so popular that he returned to Redpath-Vawter for 1912 and 1913 before moving to another circuit. The band, which was based out of Chicago, played year-round at a variety of venues.

The Weatherwax Quartet, four brothers from Iowa, performed on chautauqua circuits for many years. On Vawter's 1911 circuit the quartet performed in towns one day before the Clarke-Bowers Company, so the two groups met occasionally.

The Heimerdinger Entertainers provided a musical and literary program. Alma Heimerdinger was a prominent platform reader who performed on chautauqua and lyceum circuits for many years.

The Riner Sisters were with C. Edward Clarke on a lyceum tour in 1910 and 1911 and performed on the chautauqua circuits for several years. The two sisters, Imogene and Marguerite, looked alike and dressed in similar clothes for their performances, which included a variety of activities.

MUSIC
SOMETHING NEW
DAILY

THAVIU, the Russian Bandmastre, with his *International Band* of thirty players and *Grand Opera Stars* will furnish two of the richest musical extravaganzas ever offered to a Chautauqua audience.

THE CLARKE-BOWERS COMPANY is a combination of artists whose selections will consist largely of the more classical music and make their strongest appeal to those of more critical taste.

THE DUNBAR SINGING ORCHESTRA is the latest product of the famous organizer, Mr. Ralph Dunbar. It is composed of six winsome and versatile girls rendering programs of rare beauty.

THE WEATHERWAX QUARTET of singers and trumpeters represents the best modern conception of what a Male Quartet ought to be. Vigorous, ambitious, talented, versatile, they fill the bill to the last word.

THE WHITE ROSE ORCHESTRA under the direction of J. Howard Holt, is a family of seven trained musicians. They feature a Full String Orchestra, Chorus of seven voices, Ladies' Quartet, Mixed Quartet, Instrumental Solos, Duets and Trios.

THE HEIMERDINGER ENTERTAINERS, headed by that Queen of Readers, Miss Alma Heimerdinger, present programs of great variety and are prepared to do just what their name implies, to give preludes that will entertain.

MR. PUGH AND THE RINER SISTERS form a trio of exceptional merit, whose active, catchy and popular work will afford a world of merriment and close in a blaze of glory seven exceptionally strong musical days.

This is one of the pages from the 1911 Redpath-Vawter brochure. In the middle photograph is C. Edward Clarke. The chautauqua organization printed a largely standardized brochure for each of the towns. The cover and daily program pages were individualized. There was also one page for the local chautauqua committee to describe the town. Redpath Chautauqua Collection, University of Iowa.

OPPOSITE BOTTOM:

LEFT: In addition to the musical part of the program, William Weatherwax usually recited "Essay on Grass," in which he imitated the voice of a young boy. The *Adams County Free Press* (August 9, 1911) commented that the essay "simply convulsed the audience." Ruth took this picture of William practicing his routine.

RIGHT: The Weatherwax Quartet sang and played the trumpet, and their signature song was "The Little Brown Church in the Vale." This poster was produced a few years after the 1911 circuit. Redpath Chautauqua Collection, University of Iowa.

TOP LEFT: A.F. Thaviu, left, with chautauqua supervisor Julius Rohde. Rohde, who had been the manager for the Ramos Spanish Orchestra, sent Ruth a copy of this picture, and she put it in her photograph album.

TOP RIGHT: A.F. Thaviu's band was the largest and most expensive musical group on the chautauqua circuit and it was supplemented by a small company of grand opera singers who were part of the evening program. This postcard of Thaviu is part of a set that Redpath-Vawter produced in 1911. Alfred Moredock Papers, University of Iowa.

TOP: Ruth took this picture of the Weatherwax brothers outside the small chautauqua tent where the performers got ready for their program. Left to right: Asa, William, Lester and Tommy.

BOTTOM: Ruth photographed the Dunbar Singing Orchestra with supervisor Oliver E. Behymer.

As noted in the chautauqua brochure, the Dunbar Singing Orchestra was "the latest product of the famous organizer, Mr. Ralph Dunbar." Dunbar was an impresario who for many years successfully organized musical groups that played on chautauqua circuits. He emphasized his ability to provide music that was between the popular and classical extremes. Both postcards are from the Alfred Moredock Papers, University of Iowa.

several different speakers in that time slot. Normally, the evening lecturer with the Clarke-Bowers Company was Arthur K. Peck, who presented a program called "Storm Heroes of Our Coasts." On Sunday the musical program usually included some religious songs.

Almost all of the Iowa newspapers provided detailed coverage of the chautauqua programs in their communities. The description of chautauqua week and the performers in Hampton, Iowa, by the *Franklin County Recorder* is typical. The article (slightly abridged here) discusses the value and importance of this event and is a good example of the style and language of Iowa community newspapers of that era.

> The Hampton Chautauqua, conducted for the fifth consecutive year under the management of the Redpath-Vawter System, closed last night with a record for attendance that exceeded all expectations. It has been a seven days' feast of lectures, music and pictures, trained animals and birds. The weather could not have been better if made to order. Every session found the large tent packed with people who came to listen and learn. The program included many of the best lecturers in the country and some of the finest musical organizations, with other features that added zest and interest. Each session contained something that contributed in no uncertain way towards better things and higher ideals.
>
> The Chautauqua opened last Wednesday afternoon with a musical entertainment by the Dunbar Singing Orchestra, composed of half a dozen winsome and versatile girls, who sang and played with an attractiveness that could not fail to please. The lecture was delivered by Walter Mansell. His subject was "The Other Fellow" and he spoke to the point and crowded his address with matter of interest to live people. He is a man who tells in a strong way of the lofty elements of good citizenship. Wednesday evening the audience enjoyed another fine program from the Dunbars and then came Thomas McClary with his lecture "The Mission of Mirth." It was a talk on mirth and its connection and association with good health and the other things that go to make up what is worthwhile in this life ...
>
> Thursday the Weatherwax Quartet, consisting of four young men, furnished the music, both afternoon and evening. They are not only singers but musicians as well and their trumpet work was out of the ordinary. The afternoon lecture, "Old Days in Dixie," given by Miss Belle Kearney of Mississippi, was a fine talk on the historical conditions of the south from the time of the coming of the Cavaliers from England up to the present... William Jennings Bryan gave the evening lecture and the

immense crowd that greeted him proves beyond a doubt that Bryan is still a drawing card ...

On Friday the Clarke-Bowers Company furnished an abundance of splendid music. The Company is composed of only three members, Mr. Edward Clarke, Miss Ruth Bowers and Miss Grace Desmond, but each one is an artist. Mr. Clarke is both a singer and an elocutionist. Miss Bowers delighted everyone with her magnificent work with the violin and was forced to answer to encores after every number of her part of the program. Miss Desmond at the piano showed her ability on the instrument. Mr. James Francis O'Donnell was the afternoon lecturer and he is a monologist without a peer. His selection was "The Sign of the Cross." The play is taken from the history of Rome...The evening program was exceptionally interesting and a large audience

DR. WILLIAM EDGAR GEIL—Lecturer

Dr. William Edgar Geil is one of the world's foremost explorers. He has traveled extensively in almost every continent of the globe and all the while with both eyes wide open.

He has crossed China five times. He traversed the entire length of the Great Wall. He visited the pigmies of Congoland and learned their ways.

He has witnessed the barbarities of savagery. He has seen man-eating cannibals roast human flesh. He has had many hairbreadth escapes from violence or death at the hands of savages. Only his immense size and strength saved him.

As a result of wide travel and carefully noting important discoveries, Dr. Geil has the richest collection of travel lore of any human being. And he has a happy and clear cut way of presenting it on the public platform that makes it a double delight to hear him.

JAMES FRANCIS O'DONNELL—Lecturer

James Francis O'Donnell will present in Monologue that thrilling and dramatic story "The Sign of the Cross," one of the strongest portrayals of the tragedy of Rome and the power of love ever conceived.

O'Donnell stands in the very front rank as a monologue artist and brings into the piece so much reality that his own personality early fades from view. Only the actors in the lurid tragedy remain.

The "Sign of the Cross" depicts some scenes in the burning of Rome by Nero. All the frightful expressions of heathen hatred of Christians is brought out. The terrible price of ancient Christian faith is clearly shown.

The tenderer part of the thrilling tragedy is the pretty thread of love and heroism combined in the lives of two of the actors. Throughout the recital, however, there is a sustained and substantial interest.

HON. ARTHUR K. PECK—Lecturer

Hon. Arthur K. Peck brings to the Chautauqua a most interesting and instructive treatise on the Government Life Saving Service.

Mr. Peck has collected for this occasion the finest imaginable illustrations. These are thrown upon a large screen by a stereopticon and illustrate every phase of the subject.

But the features of most thrilling interest will be the superb motion pictures showing storms at sea; ships in distress with sailors lashed to the rigging; rescue scenes of nearly drowned sailors being dragged through the surf by means of the breeches buoy; wreck-strewn coasts and similar pictures of storm desolation.

Mr. Peck spent years of his life in the Life Saving Service and speaks from practical knowledge and experience. His lecture will be a delightful combination of entertainment and instruction.

This brochure page describes some of the lecturers. Redpath Chautauqua Collection, University of Iowa.

was splendidly entertained by Hon. Arthur K. Peck who gave his lecture on "Storm Heroes of Our Coasts" which was illustrated with beautiful views and most excellent moving pictures.

Saturday the White Rose Orchestra was scheduled to furnish the music and the most that can be said for them is that they did the best they could, but truth compels us to remark that they were disappointing. The afternoon audience, however, were royally entertained by a splendid lecture from Dr. William Edward Geil who is an explorer and traveler. He has spent a considerable time in Africa and it was on that part of the globe that his lecture, "A Giant in Pigmy Land" was based... The evening lecture by Hon. Joseph Folk of Missouri, who spoke on "The Era of Conscience" was received with great enthusiasm. Mr. Folk is a well-known reformer and a fighter and the world likes a fighter, especially one who wins, and he is of that kind.

Sunday was the banner day in attendance for the reason that everybody could be there and the further fact that Thaviu's International Band was here. In the afternoon this splendid organization was heard in a grand musical festival and in the evening the band gave another concert, followed by the rendition of a portion of the grand opera, "Cavaliera Rusticana" by four singers who knew how to sing and sing right. Thaviu's great orchestral band gave the people at the Chautauqua Sunday the finest treat in the music line that has ever come to this city. In the afternoon, following the band concert, Bishop Robert McIntyre, of St. Paul, delighted the large audience with his lecture "Buttoned Up People," and fully sustained his reputation as a philosopher, genius and orator.

Monday the Heimerdinger Entertainers took charge of the musical portion of the program and pleased. In the afternoon Garetta and his collection of animals and birds made a hit with the kids and the older people as well. Garetta has accomplished almost the impossible with the birds. He makes them do everything but talk. Prince, a dainty Shetland pony, also came in for a generous amount of attention. Monday evening James L. Lardner delightfully entertained a large audience with a lecture recital on "Riley and the Common People," which consisted of a critical study of the great Hoosier poet, interspersed with choice gems from his works.

Yesterday (Tuesday) the closing day, was among the best of the week. In the afternoon Dr. Charles Seasholes, of Philadelphia, delivered his great lecture, "The Man with the Pick." His talk abounded in humor and pathos — nicely interwoven — and filled with rich philosophy and good cheer. The musical end

Program

LE MARS

July 11 to July 17

J. R. ELLISON
Superintendent

ELEANOR MILLER
Morning Hour Lecturer

Programs Begin Promptly

Scouts 9:00 a.m. Morning Lecture 10:00
Afternoon Music 2:30 Afternoon Lecture 3:00
Evening Music 7:30 Evening Lecture 8:15

TUESDAY

AFTERNOON—Opening Exercises and Important Announcements
Music by DUNBAR SINGING ORCHESTRA
Popular Lecture
"The Other Fellow"   DR. WALTER MANSELL
EVENING—Concert by   DUNBAR SINGING ORCHESTRA
Humorous Lecture
"The Mission of Mirth"   THOMAS McCLARY

WEDNESDAY

"Scout Camps" for the Children
Morning Lecture—"American Literature"
AFTERNOON—Music by   WEATHERWAX BROS. QUARTET
Popular Lecture
"Old Days in Dixie"   MISS BELLE KEARNEY
EVENING—Concert by   WEATHERWAX BROS. QUARTET
Monologue
"The Sign of the Cross"   JAMES FRANCIS O'DONNELL

THURSDAY

"Scout Camps" for the Children.
Morning Lecture—"American Literature"
AFTERNOON—Music by   CLARKE-BOWERS COMPANY
Address by   BISHOP WM. A. QUAYLE
EVENING—Concert by   CLARKE-BOWERS COMPANY
Lecture (Illustrated) Beautiful Slides and Motion Pictures
"The Passion Play"   HON. ARTHUR K. PECK

FRIDAY

"Scout Camps" for the Children
Morning Lecture—"American Literature"
AFTERNOON—Music by   THE WHITE ROSE ORCHESTRA
Travel Lecture
"A Giant in Pigmy Land"   DR. WILLIAM EDGAR GEIL
EVENING—Concert by   THE WHITE ROSE ORCHESTRA
Lecture
"The Era of Conscience"   HON. JOSEPH W. FOLK

SATURDAY

"Scout Camps" for the Children
Morning Lecture—"American Literature"
AFTERNOON—   THAVIU'S INTERNATIONAL BAND
In Grand Musical Festival
EVENING—Musical Extravaganza GRAND OPERA COMPANY
Accompanied by Thaviu's Band

SUNDAY—Afternoon

AFTERNOON—Music by   HEIMERDINGER ENTERTAINERS
Lecture
"Buttoned Up People"   BISHOP ROBERT McINTYRE
Vesper Services 4:30 p. m.
EVENING—Concert by   HEIMERDINGER ENTERTAINERS
Lecture
"The Battle Against Vice"   HON. FRANCIS J. HENEY

MONDAY

"Scout Camps" for the Children
Morning Lecture—"American Literature"
AFTERNOON—Music by   PUGH-RINER COMPANY
Novelty Entertainment
GARRETTA with his Trained Animals and Birds
EVENING—Concert by   PUGH-RINER COMPANY
Popular Lecture
"The Man with the Pick"   DR. CHARLES L. SEASHOLES

Le Mars Program. Redpath Chautauqua Collection, University of Iowa.

of Tuesday's program was in the hands of the Pugh-Riner Entertainers, and to say that they made good is putting it mildly. The Company is four in numbers and Mr. Pugh and the Riner sisters are decidedly clever musical artists and not at all slow when giving comical readings. Their program afforded merriment galore.[45]

The newspaper noted that the businessmen of the community had already booked the chautauqua to appear in Hampton in 1912 by providing a guarantee of eight hundred tickets at two dollars each.

The Clarke-Bowers Company met in Chicago on June 24. They had a few practices before leaving for West Liberty, Iowa, on the afternoon of June 27. The following day they began the season there.

Among the many programs during chautauqua week, there was a wide variation in the emphasis on entertainment and education. Some performers believed that their main role was to entertain the audience, while others stressed the educational aspect of their program. In the program advertisements, the members of the Clarke-Bowers Company were described as presenters of classical music or masters of voice and violin. All three were musicians who wanted to play classical music. At the same time, the Clarke-Bowers Company had to choose selections that would make a connection with the audience. The *West Liberty Index* described their performance:

> A combination of unfortunate situations made the Wednesday afternoon concert by the Clarke-Bowers Company less of a success than it might otherwise have been. Superintendent Ellison's announcement, almost a warning, that the music was to be extremely classical prepared the audience for something they feared they could not enjoy. Classical music is appreciated in West Liberty by probably a larger majority than may be found elsewhere outside the metropolitan centers where it is offered as a steady diet, and when the Clarke-Bowers program opened it was found to contain numbers of which the most unschooled need have no fear. Good music it was, offered by artists, but unhappily it did not continue long enough to overcome the aversion which had been built against it before it began. And with this fact was the too apparent belief of the members of the company that they were condescending to play before the West Liberty audience. But they were musicians, better than many. Miss Bowers gave violin numbers which clearly demonstrated her complete mastery of the instrument and delighted her audience so far as they dared be delighted. In no less manner Mr. Clarke sang his several numbers, the encores demanded proving his reception. Miss Desmond as accompanist did not mar but rather added to the offerings of the others.[46]

It's unknown whether other people shared the reporter's perception, or whether the Clarke-Bowers Company realized that they were not relating to their audience, but this comment does not appear in any of the other newspaper reports. Ruth often talked about how much people enjoyed hearing classical music and how she liked playing to these audiences. In the era before radio and television, the chautauqua program was one of the few opportunities for people in rural communities to hear classical music played by professional musicians.

From West Liberty the Clarke-Bowers Company traveled to Cedar Rapids, the headquarters of the Redpath-Vawter Chautauqua, where the program was held on the grounds of Coe College. In an article on June 30, the *Cedar Rapids Republican* described the chautauqua program of the previous day in great detail:

> Yesterday afternoon a new member was added to the Clarke-Bowers Company when they appeared at the Chautauqua. The new member was a little sparrow. While Superintendent Graham was introducing the company to the audience the little sparrow alighted on Miss Bowers' shirt waist. Mr. Clarke noticed it and dubbed it a new member of the company.
>
> It was another excellent program that the Chautauqua audience listened to yesterday afternoon. It was backwards in a way. Instead of the lecturer being the last number as usual, he was first in order that he might catch a train.
>
> As it was he only had about four minutes to catch it and some of the ladies at the Chautauqua were heard making small wagers on whether he would catch it or not.
>
> Mr. James Francis O'Donnell was the lecturer yesterday afternoon. The Clarke-Bowers Company furnished the music. Both were good.
>
> Mr. O'Donnell is a monologist probably without a peer in the United States. Yesterday his selection was "The Sign of the Cross." "The Sign of the Cross" is not a comedy. Instead it is a drama of the strongest kind. Throughout its interpretation Mr. O'Donnell takes a number of parts.
>
> The play is taken from the history of Rome at about the time of the burning of that city. It portrays in a realistic way some of the things the martyrs of that day underwent as the price of Christian religion. All the hatred of the Romans against the Christians was shown in a forceful manner.
>
> Mr. O'Donnell, early in the portrayal of the play lost his personality. As soon as he had become fairly started on the monologue the audience forgot that they were listening to only one person. The different actors in the play entered upon the platform and left as though they were not creations of Mr. O'Donnell's acting.
>
> When he finished this monologue it was a couple of seconds before the audience awoke from the deep interest they were in regarding the theme of the play. When they did a ripple of applause started in the back of the tent and finally swelled to a tumult as Mr. O'Donnell left the platform.

It was one of the most impressive parts of a program in the history of the Chautauqua in Cedar Rapids. Many remarked on it afterwards. Mr. O'Donnell will certainly be extended an invitation to return to this city and repeat his monologue.

Clarke-Bowers Company, consisting of Mr. Clarke, baritone, Miss Bowers, violinist, and Miss Desmond, pianist, gave a thirty minute entertainment.

Miss Bowers opened the program with the violin rendering a Hungarian waltz accompanied by Miss Desmond on the piano. In answer to the encore which greeted this she played "Home Sweet Home."

Mr. Clarke sang several selections opening with "My Treasure." He was given hearty applause.

Miss Bowers then played Schubert's "Serenade" and responded to several demonstrations by the large audience.

Mr. Clarke closed the program with two selections, "Sound Argument" and "Gypsy Dan." The program was well rendered and greatly appreciated by the large audience.

The evening program was exceptionally interesting and a large audience was present to hear Hon. Arthur K. Peck lecture on "Storm Heroes of Our Coasts." The lecture was illustrated with beautiful views and the most excellent motion pictures of the coast that have ever been witnessed by this city. He pictured the terrors of the sea, its force and the great heroism that marks every ship wreck off our coasts.

He dwelt mostly upon the small pay that is received by the men in the employ of the life saving service. Their hardships and when they become too old for the service, how they are cast out, too old possibly to find other means of earning a living and without a pension. Or if a man loses his life while in the service his widow, if he leaves one, is perhaps one of the fortunate ones to receive possibly a year and in a few cases two years pay.

The Clarke-Bowers Company furnished the music of the evening and it may be said without the least exaggeration that they were the best that have ever come to this city on the Chautauqua platform. The company is composed of three members, Mr. C. Edward Clarke, Miss Ruth Bowers and Miss Grace Desmond. Each one is an artist. Mr. Clarke is a teacher of singing in Chicago. He has studied under Jean de Reszke of Paris and his singing is surely a credit to that great teacher. Not alone is he a fine singer. He is an elocutionist of no mean ability and the feeling

OPPOSITE: James O'Donnell.

that he can put into his songs is as readily felt in his readings.

Miss Bowers delighted everyone with her magnificent work with the violin. The instrument almost spoke under the touch of the bow and she was forced to answer to encores after every number of her part of the program.

Miss Desmond at the piano showed her ability on that instrument when she accompanied the other two members of the company in all their numbers. She was in sympathy with the soloist at all times and when she played two solos the expression that she put into the touch and the tone of the piano were a further proof of her skill.[47]

Ruth wrote to her mother describing the beginning of the chautauqua circuit.

Yesterday was our big day! We got to Cedar Rapids late Wed. eve—went to the Montrose, slept until late Thurs. morning, went to the office to see Mr. Vawter who was very pleasant to me and was driven to the Chautauqua in a big machine (wore my black & white [dress] in the aft). There was a large crowd there and our program went fine. Met the musical critic (who used to be head of the music dept of Ann Arbor) who seemed very much pleased with our program. Just as Mr. Graham was getting thru with the announcements the dearest little bird flew up and lighted on my waist. It created quite a bit of excitement and people afterwards told me that was a good omen. (I hope so.) Who do you think came to hear me? Mr. Whitesides, one of last year's Supts. Did I tell you that Belle Kearney and Dr. Seasholes are on the program this year. [They were also on the 1910 Lincoln Chautauqua circuit.] We met quite a few lyceum people and had a dandy time (went to moving picture show, lemonade, ice cream, etc.) after the program which we gave to about 1800 people and the concert was a great success. I was so glad for Vawter was there.

Ruth described the structure of their programs. "The work is easy. In the aft we fill only a half hour program before the lecture, then we have all the rest of the aft (3:30 until 7:30) to ourselves. In the eve we give an hour program—so you see we are not overworked. It is surely hot on the platform these roasting hot days, but it doesn't last for long. We three stay on the platform during the entire program. It is very similar to last year only on a larger scale."

OPPOSITE: Arthur Peck.

She also mentioned the other members of the company. "Mr. Clarke gives a nice collection of songs and sings beautifully. I like him very much. He is courteous and pleasant and full of fun. Grace is a dear…She is an excellent pianist and accompanies dandy."

The Clarke-Bowers Company spent the next week playing in towns in the Cedar Rapids area. On the last day of June, they performed at Belle Plaine. In her notes, Ruth wrote: "After the concert took a walk and landed in a swing in somebody's yard. Picked berries." June had been very hot in Iowa and Cedar Rapids, and several other towns set temperature records for that month. The warm weather continued into early July. On July 1, the company played at Grundy Center. Besides the programs, Ruth wrote, the company "did nothing but sit on the porch and try and keep cool. Intense heat—100 on the hotel porch." In the afternoon she took an automobile ride and drove past the home of James Wilson, the Secretary for the Department of Agriculture in the United States cabinet.

From Traer, Ruth sent a letter to her mother:

> I am thru with the Sun aft show. The Chautauqua here at Traer is in a beautiful big grove, regular town park with its bandstand, dancing pavilion, flower beds, ice cream stands, etc. This is actually the hottest weather I ever experienced. Yesterday it was 100 in the shade. Hot! Oh, it is terrible. But cheer up, there are clouds appearing and perhaps it will rain. Mr. Rohde is Supt of the Chaut here, it seemed real good to see him again. Did I tell you about the system? They have a crew of six men on the grounds all the time besides the Supt. I guess I told you we are apt to have a different lecturer every aft, but I expect Mr. Peck will be with us every eve. He is one of the most interesting men I have ever met. He has traveled all over the world and is such an excellent conversationalist and yet so jolly …
>
> You should see me now sitting on the grass with Grace, Mr. Clarke and Peck. They are telling funny stories, so if this is somewhat in bunches you will know the reason. We have to get up at 4 a.m. tomorrow morn. Isn't that awful!

On July 3, the Clarke-Bowers Company played at Independence, and Ruth described her leisure time there: "Grace, Miss H, Mr. Heege, Mr. Allen and I took a long auto ride in evening. Met Mr. Allen who took me canoeing in the afternoon up the river to the country club."

The Clarke-Bowers Company celebrated Independence Day, "another sweltering day," at Manchester. After their evening concert, Ruth "took a

Ruth and Keith Vawter.

glorious boat ride with Mr. C. and Grace on the river. The night was ideal and we sang and spent a dandy evening with pop and melted chocolates."

At Waverly on July 5, Ruth mentioned the heat again.

> You ought to see Grace and I. She is washing handkerchiefs and I am sitting under the window arrayed in my nightgown trying to keep cool!

Clarke-Bowers Company en route. Left to right: Grace Desmond, C. Edward Clarke, Ruth Bowers.

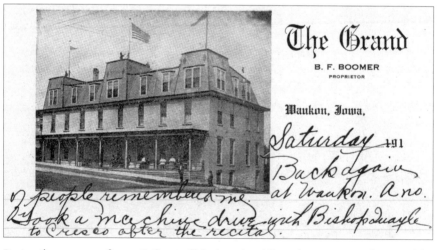

During the summer of 1911, Ruth cut off the letterhead from the stationery of many of the hotels where she stayed and used it to write notes about the tour.

I presume you have had the same scorching weather as we have had here so it is needless to say how we have suffered! I never have suffered so from heat in my life and have only existed by drowning myself in lemonade and ice cream—but even at that I have barely kept alive...

Our program is taking well in spite of its serious nature (classical, ahem). Grace is an ideal pianist and I like her personally very much so once again I'm thrown in with fine people.

Then Ruth, Clarke and Desmond headed to northern Iowa, playing at Osage the next day. "Dandy hotel! [The Cleveland.] Big crowd at Chautauqua. Mr. C. and I took a long walk. Grace was entertained." At New Hampton, Ruth noted that it was "dreadfully hot!" On July 8 the Clarke-Bowers Company performed at Waukon, in northeast Iowa, where Ruth had played in January 1910 on her first lyceum tour.

After Waukon, the Clarke-Bowers Company had the day off on Sunday, July 9, but the company had to travel to Austin, Minnesota, one of their longest trips of the summer. Ruth described the visit to Waukon and a special trip that she and Grace took.

This poster advertising the chautauqua program in Waukon could be folded and mailed. Ruth sent this to her parents.

INTERIOR
NATIONAL
FARMERS BANK
OWATONNA.
MINN.

Architect:
Louis H. Sullivan,
Chicago
Glass and Frescoing:
Louis J. Millet,
Chicago

This bank building was designed by the famous Chicago architect Louis Sullivan and built in 1908. It was the first of eight bank buildings that Sullivan designed late in his career and they are collectively referred to as Sullivan's "jewel boxes." The building is still used for banking today and is a National Historic Landmark.

July 9, 1911
Cresco, Iowa
Strother House
Sunday Special

My dear Gibby,

Nothing to do but think of you, so will scribble until dinner is ready. How did I get to this unknown burg?

This is how it happened. Last evening Bishop Quayle invited us to accompany him here so we could get a good rest today and be near our tomorrow destination (Austin, Minn) so Grace and I had a most glorious automobile ride in his big car for forty-two miles. Oh you moonlight night! But what's the use of moonlight when there is nobody around to spoon! It certainly was one of the most delightful drives I ever took. We left Waukon at eight fifteen, stopped at Decora (a town twenty miles away) for ice cream, etc., passed a stand with hot greasy popcorn—each had to have a bag, so after we had our hands full and a box of chocolates we proceeded on our way and arrived here at eleven thirty. Oh! I wish you could have been with us.

Do you remember me speaking of Mr. Rohde, the manager who accompanied the famous Ramos Spanish Orchestra on their world renowned tour of 1910? He is here today and is one of the Chautauqua Superintendents. You should have seen the reception I got at Waukon yesterday—Oh! Some class to a greeting like that, when a thousand people give you a Chautauqua salute. [A chautauqua salute was a special and infrequent tribute. The people in the audience would take out their white handkerchiefs and wave them.] They remember me from having played there before and treated me royally.

The Clarke-Bowers Company. (L to R) Grace Desmond, C. Edward Clarke, Ruth Bowers.

The Clarke-Bowers Company played at three towns in Minnesota, beginning at Austin. Ruth wrote, "Miss C., Grace and I had a late lunch and Grace ordered ice cold drinks. Chautauqua in beautiful grounds in Lafayette Park. Alas for the white roses! Had a launch ride on Cedar River with Mr. O'Donnell [the monologist], Mr. C., Grace."

While traveling from Austin to Mankato, Ruth stopped at Owatonna, where she sent a postcard of the National Farmer's Bank to her mother. "This is one of the most gorgeously colored buildings I ever saw. The whole thing is beautiful and very unique. Wait here two hours and have been filling in the time taking pictures, seeing the town and at the soda fountain."

The third concert was at Marshall. Ruth sent another postcard to her mother after her performance. "Oh you gay life! Just got to my room after playing to about a thousand people. It is nine o'clock but bed for us, have to get up at 2:30 a.m. Have had an awfully hard week's traveling. Will write later."

On July 13, the Clarke-Bowers Company returned to Iowa, playing at Le Mars. Ruth noted that while they were in the town, they were "entertained by Mrs. Freeman and her daughter Alta who is a student at New England Conservatory. The Chautauqua is in the most glorious place—a big park and grove and many people are camping on the grounds."

The *Le Mars Semi-Weekly Sentinel* described the preparations for chautauqua week:

> The seating and stage were placed and the poles set up yesterday and the canvas goes up this morning. Cleveland Park never looked prettier. In spite of the dry season the grass and trees look fresh and green and the park is in fine shape for the Chautauqua session. Campers will be more numerous than ever before, there being over thirty tents already engaged …
>
> Arrangements have been made for the policing of the grounds…[so] that the vehicles and autos outside are not disturbed. The ditches along the hitching racks have been filled recently, making a much better place to leave teams.

After their programs, the newspaper reported, "The concert on Thursday afternoon and evening by the Clarke-Bowers Company provided genuine treats and the concert ran considerably over its allotted time owing to repeated encores from an admiring audience."[48]

Advertisements like this appeared in local newspapers in advance of chautauqua week. Iowa State Historical Society.

The next day they played at Cherokee. "Had a big electrical shower today here. It is a real pretty town... The weather is ideal but we are getting up awfully early these days."

After their program in Sheldon on July 15, the Clarke-Bowers Company returned to Minnesota for one more engagement at Luverne. From the Manitou Hotel, Ruth wrote to her boyfriend.

Oh you exciting week! I have had a glorious time the past week! We have been royally entertained by bachelors, married men, Eastern Star Ladies and a girl from the New England Conservatory and have had numerous auto rides, lots of ice cream, plenty of gossip and have supped tea to my heart's content.

Have you heard of Mr. Heney, the man who investigated the San Francisco graft deal? We have been traveling with him the last two days and he is a very interesting companion, so with Mr. Peck and Mr. Clarke we are well off for male companionship.

Gibby, let me portray in elegant language the one never to be forgotten trip we took on Monday morning at 2 a.m. I assure you there was no Carnegie or shady porches but a very sleepy tired girl who boarded the train at Cresco, Iowa at that unearthly hour and who arrived at Austin, Minn., ate breakfast and went to bed.

In 1911, the automobile was not yet common in the rural Midwest. There was a mixture of automobiles and horses outside most chautauqua grounds, but each had its own parking area. Redpath Chautauqua Collection, University of Iowa.

Had another dandy auto ride this morning. Came over eighteen miles from Rock Rapids, Iowa to Luverne. It was cool and the rain had settled the dust, making everything ideal for the drive. We leave this eve. for Worthington, stay there all night, going to Sibley, Iowa at nine tomorrow morn. Had dinner with Gov. Folk this eve who is here with us—he is very pleasant personally ...

Are you having cool weather at Pgh [Pittsburgh]? The weather is ideal, the air so fresh and bracing it makes me feel great!

Nearly train time so I better cut this short and pack my grip.

In a letter to her mother, Ruth described the Sunday afternoon program at Luverne.

Have just returned from our afternoon service. I wish you could have dropped in and heard us. The tent was crowded and the program went fine. I played Holy City, Humoresque, Traumerei, Ole Bull, Home Sweet Home and Sans Parole. Mr. Clarke certainly sang gorgeously—his voice is great and he puts so much soul into his singing—so with Grace playing so beautifully at the piano we have "some music from our Company."

The day at Sibley was busy. "Oh you hot dog!!! A hard rain and hail storm at noon. Came from Worthington where we stayed all night. Met the Strollers Quartette. Had a marshmallow roast after lecture, guest of the crew. Stayed for Gov. Folk's lecture in afternoon. Had a chat with the crew and then took an auto ride."

The next stop for the Clarke-Bowers Company was at Estherville on July 18. "Rained from 4 p.m. until 8 p.m. but had a big crowd. Had a nice time with the crew boys—took pictures. Mr. Rohde Superintendent."

The concert at Forest City on July 19 was a special occasion for the members of the Clarke-Bowers Company. Ruth wrote to her mother that evening describing the event.

It's all over! But I must tell you the joke.

Our train was an hour and twenty minutes late getting to Forest City (were due at 1:20) and the exalted Clarke-Bowers Company was thrown into one auto, Hon. W.J. [Bryan] in another and I was on the platform playing Zigeunerweisen before sixteen hundred people in less time than it takes to tell about it in my green dress and red trimming, that exquisite stage gown designed by Modiste Bowers.

Oh! I feel like quite a celebrity. Bryan was so pleasant and before he left this eve he came and shook hands and wanted to know when we "next would be together."

Isn't this a dandy hotel for a town this size? They are holding a dance in the dance hall and it's maddening to hear the music and not be down there, but we have to take an early train, so "we working gals" must get to bed.

The *Forest City Summit* described this special day in their town:

The afternoon music was furnished by the Clarke-Bowers Company...Each one is an artist. Mr. Clarke is a teacher of singing in Chicago. He has studied under Jean de Reszke in Paris and his singing is surely a credit to that great teacher. Not only is he a fine singer. He is also an elocutionist of no mean ability and the feeling that he can put into his songs is readily felt in his readings.

Miss Bowers delighted every one with her magnificent work with the violin. The instrument almost spoke under the touch of the bow and she was forced to answer to encores after every number of her part of the program.

Miss Desmond at the piano showed her ability on that instrument when she accompanied the other two members of the company in all their numbers. She was in sympathy with the soloist at all times and when she played two solos the expression that she put into the touch and the tone of the piano were a further proof of her skill.

Wednesday afternoon was the banner session of the week. There were from six to seven thousand people on the Chautauqua ground, and long before the hour of the lecture all the reserved seats were taken ...

The large tent could not accommodate the tremendously large crowd that came to listen to the lecture by William Jennings Bryan Wednesday afternoon. Standing room was at a premium and Mr. Bryan once more proved himself to be one of the best drawing cards that could be put on a Chautauqua platform.

For over two hours Mr. Bryan held his hearers spellbound, and often hit the nail on the head in his recounting of past history and prophecies of reform to come...

He proved yesterday p.m. at the Chautauqua that he is the one star on the Chautauqua platform. He is the one man who despite sultry smothering weather can make men, women and little children turn out to hear him.[49]

WILLIAM JENNINGS BRYAN IN IOWA

William Jennings Bryan was the most famous lecturer on the chautauqua circuit. The politician and orator had a busy speaking schedule outside of his political career, but he always spent time during the summer delivering some chautauqua programs. In 1911, he gave a few lectures in Iowa during the last half of July. (Bryan also had a program at Independence on July 4.) Other locations besides Forest City included Woodbine, Hampton, Mount Pleasant and Denison. Bryan had a celebrity status and almost always spoke before a capacity audience in the chautauqua tent. He spoke extemporaneously for over two hours in a loud, clear voice that could be heard even outside the tent, keeping his listeners enthralled, regardless of their political affiliation.

Bryan spoke at the Woodbine Chautauqua on July 22. The *Woodbine Twiner* wrote:

> The big opening was Saturday afternoon with the great American and commoner, the man who draws the biggest Chautauqua money of any man in this country today as an attraction. A little better than twenty two hundred people passed through the gates that afternoon and saw the notable smile, the low set jaw and the scant-haired upper deck of a man whose name is a household word in every community of the United States and even beyond …
>
> He chose for his subject "The Sign of the Times" and for two hours he held his audience…Mr. Bryan looks much older than he did a few years ago, but seems to have lost none of his energy and vigor.[50]

The newspaper then discussed his lecture in detail. Bryan delivered another lecture at Denison on the same day. The *Denison Bulletin* described his appearance:

> Mr. Bryan came to Denison from Woodbine on the Illinois Central train at 6:32 Saturday evening. A number of automobiles with many of the prominent citizens of the town were on hand to meet the distinguished guest and to give him a little ride around the city before taking him to the hotel for supper. P.D. McMahon's splendid car was placed at the disposal of the committee for the use of Mr. Bryan, and with this car in the lead the others followed along the streets while people cheered as the familiar face of Mr. Bryan came into view and passed them.
>
> The Chautauqua tent was filled full long before the time of the lecture and people were there from every part of the county and for many miles around, in spite of the fact that the weather was threatening and clouds bespoke rain, and many stood outside the tent during the whole two hours of the lecture.

After describing Bryan's lecture, the *Bulletin* wrote about his concluding remarks and the aftermath of the program:

> When two full hours were up Mr. Bryan said he would close with a brief reference to the initiative and referendum and recall. These principles in government he explained in his plain and careful way so that all could understand, and in the dry discussion of such problems he held his audience spellbound with his smooth and easy flow of language until few realized that they had sat over two hours listening to one whose matchless oratory was so seductive and pleasing that another hour would have been willingly taken of his time.
>
> At the hotel after the meeting Mr. Bryan had many callers, and until eleven o'clock he talked cheerfully and freely with all who came to him, as though he were not tired with 500 miles of travel that day and with four hours and a half of platform work. He retired promptly at eleven to rise again at four in the morning when he took an early train for Lincoln [Nebraska] to spend two hours and a half with his family before he had to fly off again for other fields.[51]

This was the standard cover used for the 1911 chautauqua programs. The picture of the feature speaker for that town would be inserted in the center, and the name of the town and program dates would be printed in the white space underneath it. Redpath Chautauqua Collection, University of Iowa.

Ruth's photo of William Jennings Bryan was one of the favorites in her album.

The newspaper then provided coverage of Bryan's lecture.

To reach Northwood the next day, the Clarke-Bowers Company had to take a roundabout route through Minnesota. "Had a great time getting here. Oh you freight! At Albert Lea, Minnesota 4 a.m. until 8 o'clock. Took a machine ride in the afternoon with Mrs. Brickett. Big crowd."

After the performance at Northwood, the company had a long train trip to Hampton in southern Iowa. In a postcard to her mother, Ruth wrote: "Like this town very much, there are such beautiful homes and buildings. Played to a crowded assembly tonight, weather ideal."

The trip to Eldora on July 22 was short, but they had a long journey

Former governor Joseph Folk and Julius Rohde outside the chautauqua grounds.

Ruth and Grace in front of the tent where the crew boys stayed.

(L to R): Peck, Rohde and morning lecturer Eleanor Miller on the chautauqua stage.

afterwards to Woodbine, in western Iowa. Ruth wrote about her day in the community:

> This is a real pretty town on the Iowa River. As we got here at nine o'clock, two of the crew boys took Grace and I out on the river for a long boat ride. Had a dandy time and landed at a real pretty grove down the river about two miles. Got back here in time for dinner and gave our concert as usual at 2:30. Bishop McIntyre was [the] speaker, a real preachery sort of a looking individual but quite humorous.
>
> Have to leave here at a quarter to four a.m. tomorrow, ride six miles in an auto to Gifford and get a train there for Lake City where we arrive at 8 o'clock. Me for bed at nine o'clock if I can get there!

The company did not have any performances scheduled for Sunday, July 23, which was fortunate, especially since they had transportation difficulties. Ruth described the situation to her mother:

> I told you about having to take a machine ride part way. We took it in the worst trap of an auto…and when about half way up a hill the old [thing] broke down and we started sliding slowly down hill.

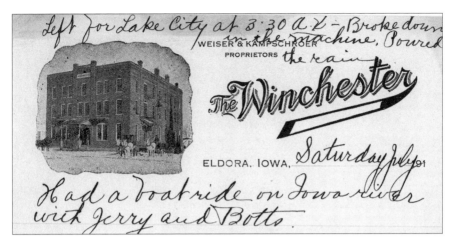

The Winchester.

Talk about frightening. Picture us in such a place on a country road at 4 o'clock a.m. with the rain coming down in torrents and only a half hour to train time. Great spot. But the driver managed to fix the old "chug-chug" and we puffed into Gifford five minutes before train time.

The company performed in Woodbine on July 24. "Had a six mile auto drive at 7 a.m. and nearly froze. Oh! You chef, Mr. Peck [chautauqua lecturer]. Peaches and cream." The following evening they played at Denison to a "big enthusiastic crowd, most responsive of any during the season." In a postcard to Charles, Ruth wrote: "Hope you don't have such cold weather for camping as we are having in Iowa. Nearly froze coming here this a.m. in a machine. This is some live town." After the performance, they had to travel to Audubon for their program the next day.

During the last days of July, the Clarke-Bowers Company played at two towns west of Des Moines, Perry and Stuart, and then traveled to Newton, east of the capital, where Ruth wrote to her mother:

This a dandy town and fine hotel but alas! We have to leave to-night as the train service in this part of the globe is awful on Sunday and we working people have to suffer!...Last night we had a melon feast at Stuart: ice cold watermelon, cantaloupe, etc. Had a good time with the Supt, Mr. Hayes a Harvard man, very pleasant. Bishop McIntyre just left us, we hated to see him go, for we all liked him so much. He recited a poem of Riley's to me yesterday—My Fiddle—and told me to always remember it when I felt discouraged with my music.

Bishop William McDowell and Peck in front of the chautauqua tent.

From Mount Pleasant, where the Clarke-Bowers Company played on August 2, Ruth sent a postcard to her mother: "This is a real pretty town. A college is located here and we had a delightful audience. Yesterday at Ottumwa had a fine time—big enthusiastic crowds, an auto ride. The hotel was good and we met some lovely people."

The headline for the *Mt. Pleasant Daily Journal* conveyed the excitement that the chautauqua programs brought to the town. The newspaper described the performance of the Clarke-Bowers Company:

> The Clarke-Bowers trio yesterday afternoon offered a number of selections that may be said to be invaluable. Miss Ruth Bowers, the violinist of the trio, displays exceptional ability upon that instrument and since all appreciate the music of violin when in the hands of an artist, she met with favor that has seldom been accredited by a Mt. Pleasant audience.
>
> Edward Clarke, the possessor of a beautiful baritone voice, surely aroused the envy of every person in that audience. Clear and melodious, and with the peculiar qualities which come to one only after years of culture and training, his renditions of several solos were hailed with the keenest delight.
>
> To Miss Grace Desmond these musicians offered no small amount of their success. Her masterful accompaniment on the

OPPOSITE PAGE (L to R): Grace Desmond, an unknown performer and Ruth.

piano impressed the audience since they could not fail to detect the perfect blending with the music of Miss Bowers and Mr. Clarke.[52]

From Mount Pleasant in southeast Iowa, there was one more long train trip to Greenfield, in the southwestern part of the state. Ruth noted: "The Chautauqua [is] situated in a big grove. Campers on the grounds. Arrived early. Had a chat with the Weatherwax boys. Had supper with Mr. Kramm and Grace was with Mr. Fuller." At Corning, where they performed on August 4, Ruth wrote to her mother describing a busy time on the circuit:

As I told you Bishop McIntyre left us Saturday and Monday at Hedrick, Mr. Frank W. Gunsaulus of Chicago joined us. Everybody in this part of the country knows him and he is second only to Bryan in popularity. He is head of the Armour Institute of Chicago and pastor of the largest congregation in Chicago, also preacher in the Auditorium (the Grand Opera Theatre) Sun afternoons.

For being such a world renowned speaker and a man of such a vast reputation he is so democratic and pleasant. Full of funny stories and experiences, he will only be here with us this week as he leaves on Monday for Chautauqua Lake, N.Y. to take charge of the lectures there. He has been fine to me and given me public praise from the platform. It is surely a great education to meet such distinguished men.

Mr. Vawter, his secretary, and the auditor have been with us all week so we have had quite a large party...

Tuesday at Ottumwa we had a fine time. It is quite a city! Stayed at a swell hotel with some lovely people who took me auto riding and the crew boys treated us.

Mt. Pleasant was a pretty place and Mr. Vawter gave us a spread on the grounds after the show...Had pie a-la-mode, apples, peaches and watermelon.

Left at 10:40 and had an all night ride to Greenfield.

The Chaut was very large and the grounds are in a big grove. About 25 tents for the campers are on the grounds. The hotel was awful and last eve Mr. Kramm, a football player of Cornell took me to supper at a private house.

The Clarke-Bowers Company spent the last four weeks of the 1911 chautauqua tour in Missouri, except for a performance in Seymour, Iowa, on August 13. In a letter dated August 11, Ruth told her mother about some of the events of the previous week.

BELLE KEARNEY AND WOMEN'S DAY

MISS BELLE KEARNEY

OF MISSISSIPPI

**Lecturer — World Traveler — Writer — Represents
Southern Aristocracy — A Slave
Holder's Daughter**

There is perhaps no woman on the platform today more popular than Miss Kearney. She has visited every state and territory, made a trip around the world, and has inspired hundreds of audiences with the highly interesting accounts of her travels.

While abroad she was entertained by royalty, and was the guest of many famous personages, including Count Tolstoi. Since she has been in Lyceum work, she has had the highest endorsement of such leaders as Judge Calhoun of the Mississippi Supreme Court, Late Senator Blair of New Hampshire, Frances E. Willard and Lady Henry Somerset.

Miss Kearney has addressed state legislatures at their request. The press unanimously calls her America's foremost woman speaker.

SUBJECTS
Old Days in Dixie Land
Woman in the Orient
Russia as I Saw It
Lights on Japan
Life in Egypt
Who is Responsible?
The Ship's Barnacles

The possibility that we may fail in the struggle ought not to deter us from the support of a cause we believe to be just; it shall not deter me. — Abraham Lincoln, Dec. 20, 1839

13

This description of Kearney is from the 1910 Lincoln Chautauqua brochure. Redpath Chautauqua Collection, University of Iowa.

Belle Kearney and Ruth were on the same chautauqua circuits in 1910, 1911 and 1912, but they were never on the same program. Born in 1863 in Mississippi, Belle was the daughter of a plantation owner who became impoverished during the Reconstruction era. Initially she attended a ladies' academy but had to quit when her father could no longer pay her tuition, so she continued by educating herself. She became a teacher and later an orator, speaking throughout the United States and internationally. Belle was one of the leading female orators of the early chautauqua tours and her main lecture topic was "Old Days in Dixie." She was an interesting mixture of white supremacist, speaker and lobbyist for the National American Woman Suffrage Association and member of as well as spokesperson for the Woman's Christian Temperance Union. Belle wrote two books. *A Slaveholder's Daughter*, published in 1900, was her best-known publication.

Several towns on the 1911 Redpath-Vawter circuit had a Women's Day and Belle was the feature lecturer. The *Adams County Press* reported on Belle Kearney lecturing for a Women's Day for the Corning Chautauqua:

The women folks will be glad to learn that we are to have a Women's Day. It is a nice recognition of the interest the women have always shown in the things the Chautauqua stands for. It will be a great day and every woman in this section of the country ought to be there. We have had many leading men on our programs; now we are to have a leading woman.[53]

The *Estherville Vindicator and Republican* wrote:

There is to be a Women's Day at Chautauqua this season. At great expense and after much persistent effort, Miss Belle Kearney has been secured for the day, and the bare announcement of her name assures the success of the occasion. Miss Belle Kearney is one of the foremost of women in this day of women's awakening. She is a world student, a world traveler and a world force...Hurray for Women's Day at Chautauqua! The women have always been in the majority of these gatherings, and this fine recognition of their interest is fully deserved.[54]

In 1924, Belle became the first female state senator in any southern state and she served for two terms.

MT. PLEASANT, IOWA.

Chautauqua Is A Continued Success

Dr. Frank Gunsaulus Delivered a Great Lecture Yesterday Afternoon.

CLARK BOWERS COMPANY ALSO MADE HIT

To-Day Is "Bryan Day" and Every Reserved Seat Has Been Sold---Tomorrow Thavius' Celebrated Band Will Give Two Fine Concerts.

Mt. Pleasant Daily Journal headline.

C. Edward Clarke, relaxing while on tour.

Four hours to wait at this wayside station. We just came back from a restaurant where we had some punk eats and having found this scrap of paper will write till the paper gives out.

Thank you, no more Missouri if I keep on suffering from the heat as I did yesterday. Oh, it was awful! I never tho't I could stand the day through. I spent the afternoon after our concert in my room in my night gown with ice on my head. The day before had been bad enough, 100^0 in the shade, but we had been staying at a private house with a nice big lawn at Albany, so we managed to exist, but yesterday at Stanberry the hotel was fierce and everything in the town was the same. I never put in such a wretched day.

The past week has been quite strenuous. Saturday morning at Corning our train was ten hrs late so we took a sixty five mile drive in an auto from Corning to Osceola, Iowa. Stopped at Creston for ice cream & fruit. The ride was thru the hilliest country, up and down the whole way and when you hear we made it in less than three hours you may know we went some.

Left Dr. Gunsaulus on Sunday and were met by Dr. Bishop McDowell of Northwestern University on Monday at Mt. Ayr. As Mr. Clarke says: "Bishops may come and bishops may go but we go on forever."…

Had my marquisette washed at Mt. Ayr. She washed it dandy and altho of course the pleats are all out and it's a plain ruffle on the bottom, it looks real nice and clean…

We met some very nice young people at Mt. Ayr and had three auto rides.

At Grant City we had a marshmallow feed after the lecture and Wed. eve at Albany had a melon spread. This is the land of the melons, they are delicious. Have also had a lot of peaches, grapes and plums.

The oppressive heat and difficulties continued through August. Grace Desmond became ill and had to leave the company, as Ruth described to her mother:

We are still existing with the weather, 101^0 in the shade—oh, it is beyond description what we went thru with on Friday, Sat and Thursday of last week. The hotels were poor, the meals were terrible and I tho't I would surely give out but I didn't and feel fine today.

OPPOSITE: Arthur Peck holds a case containing the slides for his illustrated lecture, while Dr. Frank Gunsaulus is smoking a cigar.

Dr. Frank Gunsaulaus was a preacher, humanitarian, civic leader, author, educator and, for many years, the president of the Armour Institute of Technology in Chicago. He was considered one of the most prominent lecturers on the chautauqua circuits.

It was too much for poor Grace and we fairly dragged her to Seymour on Sunday. Got her to bed in a dandy hotel. Called the Dr and found she had a raging fever of 103^0 with all the symptoms of typhoid. Monday morning she was carried to the physician's home, had a trained nurse and if able was to leave last night for Chicago. We are waiting for news in regard to her condition now. Poor girl, how I hated to leave her among strangers. I nursed her Sat night and Sun night—gave her ice baths and medicine every three hours and slept on the floor between times. You can imagine how I felt on Monday—but as soon as I got to Memphis I slept and I feel alright now.

At the end of her letter, Ruth tried to reassure her mother. "Don't worry about my health. I'm drinking lots of lime and lemonade as the Dr. directed me in order to avoid the fever and I'll let you know at once if I don't feel well, but I know I'll be alright."

Edward and Ruth hired another pianist to finish the season. Ruth wrote about their performance at Montgomery on August 23:

On Wed we were at Montgomery and experienced the most awful weather. The rain came down in torrents all day, a cold dismal pour and the tent leaked like a sieve. Oh, it was awful and we had to sit around in wet shoes and stocking[s] with the result—easy to guess—we all caught cold. Fortunately we stayed at the most hospitable, big southern home where they were giving a house party Chaut week, so had a chance to dry out when I got home, and at night the lady fixed me up a hot drink to prevent me taking cold, but alas I caught it anyway. I felt miserable on Thursday and Friday but yesterday felt fine and today feel pretty good considering I have cramps.

Ruth enjoying some leisure time with chautauqua people.

To go back to Montgomery, I wish you could have seen the real "Aunt Dina" there. There was the real old slave house back of the big house and this old darkey's family have done the work in the family since before the war. She was an old, old, darkey that was as broad as she was long, wore a yellow turban and smoked a pipe and made the best eatings and her grandchild was [the] dining room girl, a girl about fourteen with about a thousand pigtails sticking up all over her head and who rapped at our door in the morning with the exclamation—"Please ma'am, the biscuits done baked and Miss Clara (that was the lady's name, Clara Hibbert) done said get up."

One of the final programs for the 1911 season was at Warrenton. This was the first year that the town had a chautauqua program, and the *Warrenton Banner* attempted to describe the importance of chautauqua week:

The first Chautauqua for Warrenton is over, and will go down in the history of our little city as one of the most helpful and entertaining events ever held here. The excellence of the programs was far beyond the expectations of even those who were familiar with Chautauqua work. Each program seemed better than the preceding one, and when the program came to a close it seemed almost impossible that the excellence of the addresses and the music could be improved upon…

The world renowned speakers of the week gave us mountains of thought food that will require many months to digest. They gave us something to laugh about, to think about, and to cry about, and above all gave us that indescribable something that will make all who heard them better men and women.

The *Banner* also wrote about the afternoon performance of the Clarke-Bowers Company:

The selections of these artists consisted more of the classical music. Mr. Clarke had a deep full baritone voice that thrilled the large audience with the selections given. Miss Bowers, violinist, more than charmed the audience with her strains brought from the bow. For soft feeling sympathetic music, Warrenton had never before heard the equal.

Then Thomas Brooks Fletcher, who had been on the chautauqua circuit since 1906, gave his famous "Martyrdom of Fools" lecture, which the newspaper described as a masterpiece.

The *Banner* also described the evening program:

Thursday evening the Clarke-Bowers company again entertained the large audience very delightfully for one hour, after which Hon. Arthur K. Peck gave his illustrated lecture on "Storm Heroes of Our Coasts." The pictures were most magnificent. The features of most thrilling interest were the superb motion pictures showing storms at sea, ships in distress with sailors lashed to the rigging, rescues of near drowned sailors by means of the breeches buoy and other scenes of the coast. He gave an excellent idea of the great work of the Government Life Saving Service.[55]

At the program in Fayette during the last week of August, Ruth met Julius Rohde one more time. Afterwards he wrote to her: "I always enjoyed the day Clarke-Bowers were with us and I enjoyed your concert each time about the most…I hope that we may meet again. Let me know what you are doing and if you ever come out to Iowa (the good state) Mrs. Rohde and I shall be very glad to have you visit us."

On September 1, Ruth sent a postcard from Kansas City, Missouri. "Near the end now and am anxiously waiting for Mexico [Missouri].

OPPOSITE: Ruth at a ticket booth.

Ruth (Left), C. Edward Clarke, and an unknown performer spending leisure time in one of the towns on the chautauqua tour. Behind Ruth is the back side of two chautauqua posters: "Meet me at Chautauqua: Big Doings."

Will leave on the 6th September. I want to stop at Villa's and Grace's a day and will then go to Winona. My cold is about gone."

The Clarke-Bowers Company finished the 1911 season in Mexico, Missouri, on September 3, and then Ruth went to Chicago to visit Grace and celebrate the end of the tour. She wrote a letter to Charles describing the events:

> As you know we finished our season of Chautauqua last Sunday eve at Mexico, Mo. in a blaze of glory and left for Chicago at eleven that night. Had a bully good time there—were entertained for dinner and supper and took a real joy ride in the eve with Mr. Behymer, the Superintendent, a charming young Harvard man—nuf sed!
>
> Arrived at Chicago Monday morning and spent a real quiet Labor Day for I was dead tired ...
>
> Tuesday noon I went with Grace Desmond to the "Tip-Top" Restaurant for lunch after which she gave a theatre party (five females!) at the LaSalle for me. Saw *Louisiana Lou*, a musical comedy—some very good stunts in it but nothing particularly clever. In the eve Grace gave me a real party.

Their home is a regular mansion and was fixed up beautifully for the "event"—after a short musicale in which we all did stunts we proceeded to the ball room and tripped the light fantastic (how's that for style!). As the guests didn't leave till about three a.m. I didn't wake up till noon…[Grace] has recovered from her illness and although she doesn't look as well as she did earlier in the season she is rapidly recovering.

The 1911 chautauqua season was a successful one for Ruth. She had an opportunity to perform once more in a company where the focus was on music. She also had worked with Clarke as co-leader of this small company and had learned from the veteran performer.

Although the Clarke-Bowers Company was not one of the popular groups like the Weatherwax Quartet or Thaviu's International Band, they played to appreciative audiences and consistently received favorable reviews in the local newspapers for the excellence of the music they played. It was a happy summer, for the three members got along well together and enjoyed each other's company, both on stage and during their leisure time.

From the 1912 Redpath-Horner Chautauqua brochure.

THE RUTH BOWERS COMPANY
JUNE–AUGUST 1912

After her visit to Chicago at the end of the 1911 season, Ruth went to Winona, Indiana, where she wrote to Gibby:

> The annual convention of the International Lyceum Asso[cia-tion] has been in session all week and about five hundred lyceum "stars" are here. Oh! We have had a good time and ended up last night by a big banquet which lasted till 2 a.m. You remember me speaking of Bayard Robley (whom I visited in Monterey, Cal)? He has treated me royally since I've been here at Winona and has taken me to all the stunts etc. Have met a great many people (the profesh you know) whom I know, so my stay has been doubly enjoyable. This is a very picturesque place but is horribly damp and I imagine it can't be very healthful. It's very quiet and restful and contains a great many Presbyterian cranks. The lake and drives are very pretty, good hotels and beautiful homes.

She also talked about her immediate future.

> My plans for this winter are very undecided and I hardly know what I shall do. Oh these mosquitoes are awful. I'm all poisoned from their bites. I have the fever again to go to New York and study and shall see what kind of approval the plan meets with at home. Grace D. is going and I should enjoy going with her immensely.

Ruth must have met Charles Horner at this convention. Horner, who had been in partnership with Keith Vawter in the Western Redpath Chautauqua, had purchased Vawter's investment in this company so that he could start his own circuit, Redpath-Horner, in 1912. The 1911 Western Redpath circuit had covered Kansas, Nebraska, Oklahoma and Wyoming. Horner would add venues in Colorado and Texas. About ten days after the convention, Ruth signed a contract to perform on Horner's circuit during the summer of 1912. She would be in charge of her

Henry Schradrieck,

"To Miss Ruth Bowers in kind remembrance from Henry Schradieck."

own company and would be its feature performer.

Since she had a contract for the following summer, Ruth wanted to use the intervening time to further develop her talent at playing the violin. She knew that C. Edward Clarke had gone to Paris to study with Jean de Reszke, one of the premier singers of that time, in order to elevate his talent. Ruth did not have the time or money to go to Europe, but she could go to New York to study with one of the preeminent violin teachers in the country. Ruth made arrangements with Henry Schradieck in New York. Schradieck, a German violinist who had come to the United States, was considered one of the foremost teachers of that instrument in the early twentieth century.

Ruth left for New York in mid-October. On October 18, she sent a postcard from the Waldorf Astoria Hotel to Gibby with the comment: "Where I am not staying. Arrived OK this morn and was met by Miss Wycherly at whose home I am at present." During the six months that she stayed in New York, Ruth resided with the family of music director Albert Wycherly. Besides studying violin, Ruth attended some cultural and political events, which she wrote about to Gibby. In one letter he said, "You undoubtedly had a busy week between shows and dances. Would surely like to see that leap year party and suffragette affair." Ruth also performed in some programs and played at a musicale at the prestigious Waldorf Astoria.

In a letter she wrote to Harry Harrison, chautauqua and lyceum manager, in early January, Ruth commented: "I have spent the past three months in New York City under the instruction of one of the world's greatest violin masters, Henry Schradieck...Have met with great success

The Ruth Bowers Company

We are realizing an ambition of more than six years in bringing Ruth Bowers into the Middle West for this Chautauqua tour. Six years ago, it would have been impossible. Great musical artists at that time scarcely knew the Chautauqua or recognized it as a field in which their art would be appreciated. And there was much at that time to justify this conception.

Ruth Bowers, as violinist, is the Maud Powell of the Chautauqua. She has scored successes in more than three hundred of the largest cities, and has toured the continent from coast to coast and from Mexico to British Columbia. She has appeared in concert work since the age of seven years. She is a pupil of Henry Schradieck, one of the world's greatest masters of the violin, and has studied also with Franz Kohler, Otto Malms and Henri Ern.

Miss Bowers will be accompanied by Celia Fox, pianist and saxophonist. Miss Fox is a former accompanist with the Dunbar Singing Orchestra.

The Ruth Bowers Company. This description is from the chautauqua program brochure.

there and feel greatly flattered at the criticisms of the N.Y. critics. I know I have greatly improved in my playing and hope to continue to do so."

Ruth returned to Erie in April to prepare for the mid-June beginning of the Redpath-Horner Chautauqua circuit.

The Ruth Bowers Company consisted of Ruth and Celia Fox, whom she knew from the Dunbar Singing Orchestra the previous year. Celia was a versatile performer who was proficient at both the piano and the saxophone (an instrument few women played at that time), and she could also sing.

As part of their advertising, Redpath-Horner described Ruth as "the Maud Powell of the Chautauqua." Powell (1867–1920) was a famous American violinist and is considered the first American to achieve international status playing that instrument. She studied violin in Europe in the early 1880s, and one of her teachers was Henry Schradieck. Her formal concert work started in 1885, and she was a pioneer in music recording in the early twentieth century. In 1893, at almost the same time that Ruth started playing the violin, Powell wrote a paper entitled "Women and the Violin." She believed that the number of successful women violinists was small at that time because few women took up the "study of the violin with the intention of making it a life work." Powell encouraged women to become violin players and to develop their talent: "Women are especially qualified by nature to be interpretive musicians." Powell urged women to make violin playing a lifelong pursuit.

Chautauqua performers boarding a train en route to their next program.

"Women are daily becoming more serious in their motives, more earnest in making their studies something to outlast their girlhood. It is to be expected that the near future will see them availing themselves more and more of the opportunities which are before them as violinists."

Horner operated a five-day and a seven-day chautauqua circuit in 1912. Ruth was on the seven-day program, which had a format that was quite similar to the 1911 Redpath-Vawter circuit. The musicians gave a performance in the afternoon (normally called a prelude) and a longer program in the evening. The average attendance was eight hundred people for the afternoon program and one thousand for the evening performance. Usually the Ruth Bowers Company had one of their daily performances with either Byron Piatt or William Rainey Bennett, well-known chautauqua orators.

On most days (except Sunday), the Ruth Bowers Company had their other program with Eugene Laurant, a famous magician and illusionist who was on the chautauqua circuit for many years.

The season began for the Ruth Bowers Company on June 17 at Sterling in northeast Colorado. Ruth traveled to Kansas City, where Celia Fox lived, and spent a day there. The two women left on the morning of June 16 and, after a twenty-hour ride, arrived in Sterling in a rainstorm. In a letter to her mother, Ruth wrote: "After getting to bed and sleeping until 8:30 this a.m. I felt better. A lot of people are here—Mr. and Mrs. Horner, Piatt, Bennett and Laurant—minus the curled mustache. They all seem pleasant and there is no reason why we should not enjoy a good pleasant summer." For their program, Mrs. Horner accompanied Celia on her songs. Between the cold, damp train ride and the rainy weather, Ruth got a cold. Ruth also noted that her trunk hadn't arrived yet. This was the beginning of some troubles with her trunk that occurred during this circuit.

The company had a performance in Cheyenne, Wyoming, on June 19, along with Laurant's company and Byron Piatt.

En route there was a dramatic experience that was recounted in the *Lyceumite and Talent* magazine:

M.V. Arnold, one of the chautauqua personnel who went on the Pikes Peak excursion.

> While Laurant and his company and Byron Piatt were waiting for a train at LaSalle, Colorado on the 19th of June, a fire broke out in the railroad depot's beggage room near Laurant's trunk with his Witch of the Flames trunk...Piatt lost his equilibrium, also his umbrella, both of which were latterly returned to him. He saved 15 crowbars and eight excursion tickets to Pikes Peak, but it remained for Eugene Laurant to immortalize himself by running up the target ladder to the very top and rescuing alone and single handed in the midst of the death dealing flames the precious life of his trained duck "Horner." [Horner had a role in Laurant's Wizard of the Supper routine.] Total loss four dollars and eighty-five cents, fully covered by insurance.[56]

And Laurant's specially made props for Witch of the Flames, which included a large casket on a nickel-plated trestle, were saved.

The *Cheyenne State Leader* reported on the second day of the chautauqua program: "The musical company and Miss Ruth Bowers delighted her audience with some excellent violin numbers. Miss Bowers was ably assisted by Miss Celia Fox whose saxophone playing was well received."[57] Then Ruth and Celia traveled south through eastern Colorado. Ruth sent a postcard from Fort Collins on June 20:

Glad to receive your letter yesterday. The scenery is beautiful around here as we get a great view of the Rockies. The concert here is held in the chapel of the College. The buildings are all great and surroundings pretty. This is quite a town. My cold is better.

During their week of traveling through eastern Colorado, Ruth and Celia were part of the group that went on the excursion to Pikes Peak. After a program at Canon City, Ruth and Celia played at Lamar. The local newspaper commented on the comparison of Ruth to Maud Powell:

Rightly is Miss Bowers called the Maud Powell of the Chautauqua for her skill on the violin is par excellent. She fairly made the violin talk, and the tones she obtained were wonderful. Miss Bowers' entertainment was a rare treat for the people of Lamar in high class music. Miss Fox showed remarkable piano ability and her saxophone selection pleased the audience very much.[58]

From Colorado, the Ruth Bowers Company traveled to the famous frontier town of Dodge City, Kansas, where they played on June 27.

EUGENE LAURANT

Eugene Laurant was the stage name for Eugene Greenleaf. Born in Colorado when it was still a territory, Laurant became a professional magician in 1896 at the age of twenty-one and began performing on chautauqua and lyceum circuits around 1905.

Although Laurant's program did not follow the chautauqua ideal of education and enlightenment, he was very popular with the audience and was considered one of the stars of the 1912 Redpath-Horner circuit. Laurant's program, titled "New Mystic Creations," created some scheduling difficulties for Horner. Most communities believed that Sunday was a sacred time and they did not want a magician performing in their town on that day. Horner's solution was to schedule Laurant for a

Laurant, Illusionist

This is the most mystifying feature any Chautauqua has ever presented.

Laurant is unquestionably the peer of all illusionists. He has brought together the weird and curious tricks from India, Egypt, Turkey, Persia, China and Japan and from throughout the Orient where illusions are not only a superstition but a religion as well.

His program this summer is entirely new, with a Chautauqua adaptation. It will last for a full hour and a half and among the big features will be the Wizard's Supper, and his new beautiful mystery, entitled "Carmen's Tambourine," culminating in a marvelous patriotic display of the world's national banners.

Laurant has two assistants, a pianist, Mr. Gradolph, and stage manager, Mr. Stigler. He carries twelve trunks of "mystic" paraphernalia.

It will be the big night for the children —the most wonderful series of surprises they have ever seen. They are asked to crowd right up in the front of the tent.

This description of Laurant is from the chautauqua brochure.

Monday-morning children's program at the town where he was scheduled for Sunday and then have Laurant perform at his regularly scheduled venue Monday evening. Horner would have a second speaker to talk about a religious topic on Sunday. Occasionally, Laurant would give performances at two towns on Saturday and Horner would adjust the schedule of his talent accordingly.

In the program brochure, Laurant is described as an illusionist, even though most of his program was about magic. His two assistants, large collection of paraphernalia, and ninety-minute program added to his allure. The chautauqua circuits were primarily for adults, but they had morning programs for children, and if the children were to become part of the future audience, the circuits needed to have one program that was suitable for the entire family. On the 1911 Redpath-Vawter circuit, there was Garetta and his trained animals; on the 1912 Redpath-Horner there was Laurant.

One part of Laurant's performance was a chapeaugraphy routine (chapeau is the French word for hat). The performer would use a ring of felt with a hole in the center that could be twisted into various hats, putting on each hat and assuming the personality of the person being portrayed. Laurant did the comment for his chapeaugraphy routine in rhyming verse.

Laurant was on the chautauqua circuits for about twenty years and is generally considered to be the best magician/illusionist that performed with them. He was elected to the Society of American Magicians Hall of Fame.

LAURANT
In Lightning Character Impersonations

LEFT: In 1913, Ernest Gradolph, one of Laurant's assistants, sent Ruth this postcard: "Do you remember the stunt pictured on the reverse side?" In the center of the postcard is the ring of felt that Laurant used for his routine. The pictures around the center are some of the personalities that Laurant would create. Chapeaugraphy is an art form that is seldom seen today.

BELOW: Ruth became friends with Laurant during the 1912 tour and took this picture of him enjoying a humorous moment.

Time 's About Up

This is the last week—the last few days before the Chautauqua starts.

Time is about up for those who are "thinking" about buying the ticket—the season ticket, that is.

You will want to be in line the first day in this procession of community folks.

You will like this first day's program. You will want, then, to go all week.

The season ticket is what you will want. It admits to the whole affair—every number—every feature of this Big Week.

There will be no extra charge once you are in.

The cost is about 15c a number on this season ticket plan.

A band from Italy and six other great musical companies—a whole list of Chautauqua celebrities a week long.

The Junior Chautauqua—a big feature for boys and girls.

Get the season ticket TO-DAY.

The Chautauqua Starts . . Last a Week . . June 26

The. Fraternity Glee Club

Ruth Bowers

The Rawls

Celia Fox, Saxophonist with the Ruth Bowers Company

A newspaper ad for the program at Dodge City. Kansas Heritage Center.

The *Dodge City Globe* wrote:

> The Ruth Bowers Company, with her accompanist, Miss Fox, gave a number of beautiful selections on the violin. She is a player of exceptional ability and her selections pleased the large audience. Miss Fox, with Mrs. W.B. Miller at the piano, rendered an excellent saxophone number and responded to an encore."[59]

The next day, Ruth and Celia played at Newton in central Kansas. The *Newton Journal* reported on Ruth's playing: "It is marvelous how the squeaking, rasping tones of your neighbor's fiddle are transformed into

Ruth collected a brochure when she was at Dodge City.

such melting mellifluent strains of music when the trained hands of an artist takes the instrument."[60] The Ruth Bowers Company then gave a few performances in the eastern part of the state. The *Woodson County Advocate* described the program at Yates Center on June 29:

UNLESS there is some very necessary cause for delay, the programs will start on time. The evening programs will begin early enough so as to make possible an early closing. Many of the Chautauqua's friends may wish to come in from many miles out in the country. They may feel safe in doing so, without the fear that the evening programs will "drag out" late.

THE boys' and girls' feature is a whole Chautauqua in itself. They have a "Daily Program" all their own which will be given to them the opening day of the Chautauqua. It will be a busy week for the boys and girls. Their games have been planned by the greatest playground expert that is known to-day. Every boy and girl in the community should be given an opportunity of participating in this boys' and girls' Chautauqua.

DAILY PROGRAM

DODGE CITY, KAN.

STARTS JUNE 26
CLOSES JULY 2

HOMER MARTIEN COOK, Chautauqua Manager

We are glad to announce Mr. Cook's coming as Chautauqua superintendent. This is his first connection with the Horner Chautauquas, but we know of his ability. He is to-day pastor of one of the largest churches in the Middle West, and is spending this summer in Chautauqua work in his vacation period. He was formerly president of a state normal school and a Chautauqua lecturer. He is a man of scholarship, ability, powerful personality. He is one of the greatest Bible students in the country. His coming will be a feature of this Chautauqua Week.

SEASON TICKETS
Adults
If purchased of Business Men . . $2.00
If purchased at Chautauqua Gate . 2.50
Childs 1.00
Single Admission—Child 15

The afternoon program will start at 2:45 o'clock; the evening program at 7:45 o'clock.
The Junior Chautauqua will be held each day of the Chautauqua under the direction of Miss Linna Bresette.

WEDNESDAY
Afternoon
Opening Exercises
Concert   The Fraternity Glee Club
Admission 25 cents
Evening
Concert   The Fraternity Glee Club
New Mystic Creations   Laurant and Company
Admission 50 cents

THURSDAY
Afternoon
Prelude   Ruth Bowers Company
Lecture   Byron Piatt
Admission 25 cents

Evening
Concert   Ruth Bowers Company
Lecture   William Rainey Bennett
Admission 35 cents

FRIDAY
Afternoon
Prelude   Harmony Concert Company
Lecture   Albert L. Blair
Admission 25 cents
Evening
Concert   Harmony Concert Company
An Evening of Fun   Ralph Bingham
Admission 35 cents

SATURDAY
Afternoon
Prelude   The Venetian Troubadours
The Sign of the Cross   James Francis O'Donnell
Admission 25 cents
Evening
Concert   The Venetian Troubadours
Sermon-Lecture   Lincoln McConnell
Admission 50 cents

SUNDAY
Afternoon
Prelude   The Novelty Players
Sermon-Lecture   Chancellor George H. Bradford
Vesper Service
Admission 25 cents
Evening
Sacred Concert   The Novelty Players
Recital   Everett Kemp
Admission 35 cents

MONDAY
Afternoon
Recital   SIBYL SAMMIS MAC DERMID
                           James G. MacDermid
Lecture   Belle Kearney
Admission 25 cents
Evening
Concert-Recital   SIBYL SAMMIS MAC DERMID
                           and James G. MacDermid
Entertainment and Illustrated Lecture   The Raweis
Admission 50 cents

TUESDAY
Afternoon
Popular Concert   ROYAL ITALIAN GUARDS BAND
Lecture   Helen B. Paulsen
Admission 35 cents
Evening
Grand Closing Concert   ROYAL ITALIAN GUARDS BAND
Admission 50 cents

The Saturday afternoon and evening lectures were full of meat for thought digestion, seasoned with wit and humor that made them most palatable.

Byron Piatt handled the subject of "American Morals" under the title of "Mating" in a most delicate, scientific and forceful manner. He urged moral instruction on the same scientific basis as intellectual and physical training. "The time is coming," he said, "when the schools of the land will inaugurate a moral

LEFT: William Rainey Bennett was a minister and dramatic orator who was on the chautauqua circuit for many years. RIGHT: Linna Bressette, a supervisor for the junior chautauqua program, later worked for the Kansas state welfare board; she was a pioneer woman factory inspector and a well-known social activist for the Catholic Church.

director the same as physical and intellectual directors. And likewise the churches are awakening to this great moral issue and are taking steps to further the movement."

Mr. Piatt has a message on his mind and heart for the American people and delivers it. He has a rich-toned voice and magnetic personality. Some flights of oratory demonstrated the earnestness of the speaker.

No artist has ever played the violin in such a highly finished manner as did Ruth Bowers in the Saturday afternoon and evening program. Her fine technical training blended with a temperament of such high artistic standard makes her rank very high in the musical world. She is a pleasing personality, with easy graces, manners and a native refinement which usually comes with a long association with the violin.[61]

Occasionally, Ruth hired a local person to play in the company for a program. The *Yates Center News* noted: "Our Miss Clara Winter accompanied Miss Fox, and we were all just as proud of her and her splendid ability as can be."[62]

After a program on July 1 in Fredonia, the *Wilson County Citizen* wrote: "Ruth Bowers, the violinist has a mortgage on the Fredonia people which she may foreclose whenever she wishes. Her work is artistic in the true sense of the word and the choice of selections was happy."[63]

The Ruth Bowers Company then journeyed south to Denton, Texas, just north of Dallas. En route they played at Pawnee, Stillwater and Guthrie in Oklahoma. The Guthrie performance was at Mineral Wells Park, the oldest historical park in Oklahoma and the site of several artesian wells.

At Denton, due to a change in the local train schedule, Laurant performed first instead of the musicians. The program also started at 2:30 instead of 3:00, so many people missed a large part of his program. The local paper reported: "The concert given by Miss Ruth Bowers and Miss Celia Fox assisted by Miss Grace Beyett of this city was delightful in every respect and received the hearty plaudits of an appreciative audience." The paper noted the "Maud Powell of Chautauqua" comparison: "Miss Bowers was particularly fine on the violin and though many years the junior of Maud Powell who played here some time ago, many thought her playing fairly the equal of that of the famous violinist." The paper also commented on the second performance: "The concert by the Ruth Bowers Company was as highly appreciated at the evening hour as in the afternoon, and Miss Bowers was forced to respond to many encores."[64]

On Sunday, July 7, the Ruth Bowers Company played at Waxahachie, Texas. Their final performance in Texas was at Gainesville, where Ruth had played in the fall of 1910, the *Daily Register* ran the following under their chautauqua program description:

RUTH BOWERS CAPTIVATED THE LARGE AUDIENCE THAT HEARD HER AT BOTH SERVICES

Yesterday was in every respect, a great day at the Chautauqua. Ruth Bowers captivated the audience, with fine interpretations of the best musical compositions.

Miss Ruth Bowers, violinist, and Miss Fox, her accompanist, were all their advance notices claim for them and more. Their program included numbers which were appreciated by the musically educated and those who were not as well. Miss Bowers played "Home Sweet Home" in a manner that made

A VISIT TO PAWNEE BILL'S RANCH

While they were in Northern Oklahoma, Ruth, Celia and Laurant visited the Pawnee Bill Ranch. Ruth told her mother that Pawnee was filled with:

> gambling joints and saloons and while we were there two men broke out of jail and we met a posse of armed men out to shoot them. Talk about your wooly west.
>
> But one thing made Pawnee liveable. We met a lovely lady who took us autoing and the next morn took us out to Pawnee Bill's home and ranch. Think of a $75,000 home out in that wilderness—a palace. The porch floor is mosaic and has buffalo pictures in the pattern.
>
> He has a herd of sixty buffalo in his ranch and we took pictures of them.

Gordon W. "Pawnee Bill" Lillie was a performer in Buffalo Bill's Wild West show for a short time before he and his wife started their own Wild West show in 1888. Pawnee Bill used his ranch to help preserve bison, which had almost become extinct. Today the ranch is an Oklahoma state historical site.

OPPOSITE PAGE TOP: A sun dance. Dancers are in the center with drummers to their right. There are advertising boards along the fence, a viewing platform and a hill in the background.

OPPOSITE PAGE MIDDLE: "This is an Indian council hut at Pawnee Bill's Ranch. Inside it is perfectly round and the covering is made of mud and sticks." L to R: Celia, Laurant, Ruth and an unidentified person.

OPPOSITE PAGE BOTTOM: Bison at Pawnee Bill's ranch.

everybody like that selection just a little better than they ever have before. Miss Bowers' home is in Erie, Penn., and Miss Fox lives in Kansas City. They are both very highly talented and good to look at.[65]

From Texas the Ruth Bowers Company traveled north to Enid, Oklahoma, for a performance. In advertising the chautauqua there, the *Hennessey Clipper* newspaper reported:

> Camping will be a big feature. A delightful place. An abundance of drinking water—provisions—everything right at hand. The grounds will be well lighted. Swimming and boating a big feature. Tents and cots at a reasonable price.[66]

A SPECIAL CHAUTAUQUA PERFORMANCE AT WAXAHACHIE

Waxahachie was one of several cities that had started their own independent chautauqua assemblies before the chautauqua circuits began. In 1902, the Waxahachie Chautauqua Park Association formed, and they organized the construction of an auditorium that could hold 2,500 people for the chautauqua assembly as well as other events. From 1902 to 1911, Waxahachie hosted an annual chautauqua that lasted about ten days and was well attended. Many people came from outside the city and stayed in tents in the park.

In a book titled *Waxahachie: Where Cotton Reigned King*, Kelly McMichael Stott provides a lyrical description of the 1912 chautauqua in that town:

> By early evening Chautauqua Park was filling to capacity. Horses were hitched to the fence around the park, swatting flies with their tails and eating the hay their owners had left for them. The campers were around their tents, the men waiting for their wives to finish dressing, laughing amongst themselves at the lengths the women folk went to for the sake of fashion.
>
> The mule street cars made regular trips from downtown and from the train terminals…Thousands converged in the park, eagerly awaiting the evening's performance. By dusk the auditorium was filled, seemingly bursting over with people …

Waxahachie Chautauqua. Waxahachie, Tex.

This is a postcard showing the chautauqua auditorium around the time Ruth performed there. The building, with its unusual architecture, still exists and is on the National Historic Register. Image courtesy of Ellis County Museum.

After the performance the sleepy children were gathered and the farm families piled back into the wagons, the ride home shortened by talk of the night's show. Over the camp, the stars glistened high in the summer sky and tiny white lights threaded through the trees mimicked the night sky. The tenters retired to their campsites, many gathering at individual fires to relive the performance.

In 1912, the Waxahachie Chautauqua contracted with Redpath-Horner to provide a circuit chautauqua program for the city. The chautauqua lasted nine days. Though most of the events came from Redpath-Horner, there were also some local activities. It was one of the few venues where a chautauqua tent was not used, and this, combined with the blend of outside and local programs, produced a unique chautauqua.

The *Waxahachie Light* commented that "the many campers are getting all the enjoyment they can out of the outing. All are comfortably situated and they have all the conveniences that could be provided for camp life and make it one continual round of pleasure." It noted that, "while the entertainment features are stronger this year than ever, the religious side of the program has not been neglected." During the weekday, this included mission studies in the morning, special religious speakers, a kindergarten program and a chorus.

The Ruth Bowers Company performed on Sunday. The two Redpath-Horner musical programs and the two lecturers were part of an entire day of activities. The *Waxahachie Light* provided a detailed description of the events.

Ruth on a mule-powered streetcar in Waxahachie. The building in the background is the Ellis County Courthouse. It is still used being used as a courthouse and is on the National Historic Register.

The newspaper reported that "Sunday was a busy day and one that was filled with many good things…The gates were thrown open free to the public and the different exercises were largely attended. Many people took their lunches and remained on the grounds until after the night sermon."

There was Sunday school in the morning, followed by a lecture sermon from William Rainey Bennett. In the afternoon, the Ruth Bowers Company performed, and then the other chautauqua speaker, Byron Piatt, lectured on the topic "The New Era Under Jesus Christ." At six o'clock there was a vesper service where Ruth and Celia played some selections. Following this, the Ruth Bowers Company performed a concert. The *Light* wrote that "Miss Bowers is a violinist of high ability and in the evening concert she was forced to respond to a number of encores. Miss Celia Fox also captivated the audience with her saxophone solos."[67] The busy day concluded with a night sermon by Dr. J. Frank Smith, who came from Dallas to speak to the audience.

The *Enid Daily Eagle* covered both of Ruth's performances and Laurant's return to the city in two articles that both began on the front page of the paper. The reporter attempted to describe an intangible effect of the chautauqua program: the personal connection between the audience and the performers.

Enid Daily Eagle
Thursday, July 11, 1912

RUTH BOWERS CO. ENTERTAIN
THEY GAVE DELIGHTFUL PRELUDE THIS AFTERNOON— LAURANT THE MAGICIAN WILL GIVE PROGRAM OF THREE PARTS

Promptly at 2:45 this afternoon Superintendent Stauffer presented the Ruth Bowers Company at the Chautauqua pavilion, and that artist and her people gave one of the very happiest and most enjoyable preludes ever heard in the park or anywhere else in the city. It was delightful and worth more than all the trouble it takes to go to the park a half dozen times to get lost with this company in a half hour of wonderful and entrancing entertainment …

LAURANT TONIGHT

It's Laurant—Laurant who was here at the Loewen last winter—who takes the boards at the Chautauqua pavilion tonight.

In this postcard that he gave Ruth, Laurant is wearing the medal that he received from the Society of American Magicians earlier in 1912.

He is on every night of the season, and is said to be in the best form ever. Something has happened to him since he was here.

Last May the society of American magicians which enrolls all the magicians and persons interested in magic who work in America held its annual meeting in New York City. This society counts among its members not only professional magicians but men of prominence as physicians, scientists and investigators in the fields of science, mystery and the occult arts.

At the meeting referred to, Laurant was presented, on the 23rd day of May, with a beautiful jeweled medal by his friends and the members of this organization. This medal was presented in recognition of the work Laurant had done in the field of research along the lines of magic, mystery and the psychic sciences. This honor has been conferred but on two other men in the history of magic, viz: Alexander [Herrmann] and Harry Kellar.

Mr. Laurant's program tonight will consist of three parts, or acts and will embrace all the latest novelties that this gifted artist has invented. Among the features will be a series of character changes made in full view of the audience with the simple rim of a hat which Mr. Laurant folds and refolds in a most interesting manner. The beautiful flower trick and the wizard supper will be interesting features also.

Enid Daily Eagle
Friday, July 12, 1912

GREAT INTEREST IN CHAUTAUQUA
RUTH BOWERS EXCELLENT

The appearance of Ruth Bowers, violinist, afternoon and evening in the preludes was something more than successful; there was triumph in both the programs and especially so in the evening. Miss Bowers really played her instrument; she wandered off with it and the audience followed, as they were able to do. The music reached the imaginative qualities of the mind, and the spirit of the player as interpreted in the varying, lingering and now flying sweet melodies and rhapsodies of the "human instrument" caught the crowd and took it captive. Miss Bowers achieved that ideal of every public person: the player escaped and left their music in the hearts of her people.

LAURANT MOST DELIGHTFUL

The last night's program was "Laurant." To him who in the love of his kind, and especially in the children, it is given to revel in their building enjoyment when lost in delightful and puzzling mystery — to him and to none other is it given to know what an evening in the pavilion means when Laurant is there. Many of the "tricks" had been seen here before, and some were as old as the earliest appearances of what used to be called sleight of hand performance, but the inimitable Laurant was there, and old things took a new form, color and interest. Laurant is Laurant, and while he is enough, he is just enough, and not a whit less enough to suit the Enid people when they think of mystery, magic, the occult manifestations and all that. So the people watched him open eyed, and often open mouthed, until all those wonder dreams of silk had been shaken into the Stars and Stripes forever.[68]

From Enid, the Ruth Bowers Company proceeded to Arkansas City, Kansas, where they performed on July 12. The *Arkansas City Daily Traveler* described the arrangements for the chautauqua program and the performers: "The advance guard with the big tent and all the paraphernalia arrived here last night from Stillwater, Oklahoma and the tent was put up today at Paris Park...The talent for the Chautauqua here will come from Enid, Oklahoma each day at noon and from here will go to Ponca City, [Oklahoma] the following morning over the Santa Fe [Railway]." The newspaper also noted the economic benefit for the community. "By this arrangement all the people who are on the program will stop here over night."[69] The newspaper recorded that the temperature was forty degrees Celsius (104 degrees Fahrenheit).

After Ponca City, the Ruth Bowers Company went to Wellington, Kansas, where they gave a program on Sunday, July 14. Since it was Sunday, Laurant did not perform, but he wrote a letter to Horner about the first part of the tour:

Our new program and my new illusion is a perfect success. I am using my new stunt making twenty characters under one hat, the last character disappears in full view of the audience. My Chautauqua program is beyond doubt the greatest I have ever produced. My assistants are doing fine work and I can safely say the show is a hit. The terrible heat however makes it very hard at times.

The *Wellington Daily News* noted the heat: "It is pretty hot in the tent in the afternoons, but then isn't it hot at home, so what's the odds as long as you are happy?"

Ruth hired local pianist Gladys Pettit for the performance in the town. She must have liked Gladys's musical talent and decided that she needed a third person for their company, for Ruth hired her. The Wellington newspaper reported on July 16: "Miss Gladys Pettit left last night to join the Ruth Bowers Company at Kingman where she will appear today as a member of the company. She will be pianist and vocalist and travel over the Chautauqua circuit the balance of the season."[70] For the remainder of the summer, Celia played part of the time with the Ruth Bowers Company and part with the Harmony Concert Company, who performed at the same venue one day later.

At Kingman, the *Leader Courier* gave an explanation for the heat inside the tent: "It is proposed to set apart a sort of parking place next year for the convenience of those who attend the Chautauqua in the automobiles, so that all will fare alike and so that the autos may not be placed up next to the tent and thus shut off fresh air and necessary cool breezes from the east, as was the case this year."[71]

One of the pieces of music Ruth played on this tour was Beethoven's Minuet in G. She received a couple of letters from admiring men who praised the way she played the minuet. One of these came from a man who heard her at Kingman.

The Ruth Bowers Company played at Pratt on July 17, and in Stafford the following day. Laurant noted that "Horner is with us today and he seems very happy over business. Big crowds have been the rule." The next town on the circuit was Kinsley, where a skeptical reporter for the *Kinsley Mercury* described his reaction to the company's performance:

> Of course we understand we are not much on music. We are not on speaking terms with sharps and flats, and we would not recognize a crescendo if we met one in the middle of the road, but some way or other Miss Bowers' productions took hold of our depraved and neglected musical construction and made us feel as much like yelling as anything does unless it's a pinch hit in a baseball game.[72]

On July 20, the Ruth Bowers Company performed at Larned and did some sightseeing. Wrote Ruth, "We had a most enjoyable trip with E.E. Frizell to the Fort Larned Ranch and saw the magnificent farm and relics of the fort."

There was a performance at Great Bend on July 21 and at Marion on July 23. The *Marion Record* reported on the company's performance and also some special information they had gathered from the chautauqua supervisor:

The cover page of a brochure about the Fort Larned Ranch.

The music on Tuesday was rendered by the Ruth Bowers Company. And it was very fine. No finer violin has ever appeared here than Miss Bowers and nothing but praise is to be spoken concerning her playing. She is a real artist. Her touch is superb and she puts soul into her tones. All her renditions were excellent, but special mention should be made of several of the old favorites — *Traumerei*, Schubert's Serenade and Humoresque. The platform manager, Mr. Beatman, says — that although he doesn't suppose that this is to be published — that Miss Bowers has been considerably annoyed for several days by the loss of the trunk containing her platform gowns. This is here said of course for the benefit solely of the men who had wondered about that.[73]

The next day, Ruth wrote to her mother from El Dorado.

Tho't you would be anxious to know that after fifteen days of worry, long distance calls and days spent in wiring I have located my trunk and have it in my possession at last.

We were just congratulating ourselves how cool it was when today we have had a scorching hot wind (only appreciated when felt in Kansas) and the heat has been 105 in the shade all afternoon. Oh! It's fine—I'm not suffering badly but poor Laurant is

A souvenir of the Great Bend Chautauqua.

suffering fierce and is afraid of a heat stroke—he fainted this aft after having taken an ice bath and had ice cloths on his head.

From Paola on July 27, Ruth told her mother:

News is rather scarce—everything is going along nicely—our programs are going great. Everybody thinks (those who have heard both programs) that Gladys is a great addition. She sings beautifully and plays so well with me. Mr. Gradolph, Mr. Laurant's assistant plays for her.

Yesterday we were entertained at Garnett at the home of a college chum of Gladys. Had a very good time and fine eats!!! The day before a friend of hers met us with an auto and took us for a nice ride.

Today is hot again but the Chautauqua is in a park and we have our cab to drive us to and from the grounds, so all is well.

For the Sunday program, the Ruth Bowers Company played a combination of sacred and popular music that always pleased the chautauqua audience. The *Wamego Reporter* recounted the program on July 28:

Gladys and a man named Muffley preparing for a performance.

The program Sunday was one especially appropriate to the day and might be fittingly called a big union service for no other religious services were held in the town. The people were given a treat in the programs rendered by Miss Ruth Bowers, violinist, who is one of the most finished artists procured for the Chautauqua, and Miss Pettit who is her accompanist, and also a sweet singer. The musical program was largely of a sacred nature, both afternoon and evening. Miss Bowers gave a repertory ranging from the most classical numbers to the simplest melodies which she knows well go straight to the heart of such an assembly as is usually found at chautauquas. So she plays for everybody, and puts into all her work the wonderful tenderness and power such as only an artist can command. Besides being a splendid musician, Miss Bowers is a charming and gracious young woman and makes a delightful impression personally upon her audience. Miss Pettit's voice is very fresh and sweet and her numbers delighted her hearers.

The afternoon lecture was delivered by William Rainey Bennett. In the evening, the order of the program was reversed, with W.C. Coleman addressing the audience first because he was leaving on the train. The *Wamego Reporter* wrote:

After the lecture the audience insisted upon playing the Oliver Twist trick upon Miss Bowers, who graciously kept responding with "more," closing her own and Miss Pettit's delightful numbers with a violin arrangement of "The Holy City," a beautiful and fitting climax. The vesper service, for which leaflets were distributed and in which everybody joined, closed the meetings for the day. Rev. F.C. Rufle of St. Luke's church pronounced the evening benediction.

The newspaper also noted Laurant's performance on Monday morning: "Laurant, the illusionist was the 'whole show,' and it was a dandy. Nothing would give us more pleasure than to explain all of his tricks but the paper will be too late this week to undertake the task."[74]

At Hays, the newspaper reported that "Mr. and Mrs. J.H. Ward had the pleasure and honor on Tuesday [July 30] of entertaining Miss Ruth Bowers the Chautauqua violinist, and Miss Fox, her accompanist, at their beautiful musical home, and it was a musical feast indeed."[75] On the last day of July, Ruth, Celia and Gladys were in Russell.

In the afternoon of Sunday, August 4, Ruth sent a letter from the Lincoln Park chautauqua grounds.

My dear Mother,
Well, such a week as we have had! I have been kept so busy I haven't found time to write. Monday at Junction City, Miss Brissette, the supervisor of children, had a picnic supper for us and we sure did enjoy it. Tues. at Hays we were entertained by a Mr. Ward, the richest man in the county...Their home was a mansion and you wouldn't believe that such a home could be out in the country in the deserts of Kansas. We had a private bath off our room, a sleeping porch and the whole house had hard wood floors and all kinds of luxuries. Their music room was one of the prettiest I have ever seen and he has a Victrola etc. Mr. Ward is a violin crank—that's how we happened to be there. Wed. at Russell we met some lovely girls who took us motoring nearly all day. Thurs. we were entertained at Ellsworth in a lovely place—they took us motoring and gave a supper in the eve.
Fri. I met a real nice fellow named Stuart, he is an advance man of Horner's, and he took me to supper. Yesterday was uneventful and today we are at Lincoln Park, an independent Chautauqua and had a crowd of 2500 people this aft. There are over 400 people camping on the grounds and we are living in a tent. I'm sitting outside our tent now writing. Mr. Laurant & Mr. Piatt are going to give us a supper tonight. They have a tent in another part of the grove.

Where the crew boys stayed.

We have had Chautauquas in the most beautiful parks for having been in such small towns and our programs are going the finest I have ever had them.

Laurant expressed a similar sentiment when he wrote to Horner at the end of July: "We are all having a fine success out here in this Dry Country. Big crowds as a rule and everything going all O.K."

Ruth concluded her letter from Lincoln Park with more unfortunate news about her trunk. "My poor trunk has had another accident. A careless baggage man punched a big traveling salesman's trunk thru it and it [has] a big hole right thru it. Grady, Mr. Laurant's man, fixed it—you ought to see the patch of tin in the side of it—some class."

Lincoln Park was a special chautauqua venue in Kansas. Located west of Cawker City at a well-known park along Oak Creek with huge oak trees and a large camping area, this was the only chautauqua in Kansas that was not in a town. Like Waxahachie in Texas, Lincoln Park had its own chautauqua for several years before 1912, and it incorporated the Redpath-Horner circuit into a larger event.

During the first week, Lincoln Park had its own chautauqua events, beginning on Sunday with church programs. Monday was Farmer's Day. Since there was a presidential election in 1912, there were two days devoted to politics, with Tuesday being Republican Day and Wednesday devoted to the Democrats. Another important issue was addressed on Thursday, Equal Suffrage Day. Friday was Old Soldier's Day. On Saturday, the seven days

This postcard shows a gathering at Lincoln Park. Ruth noted that there were 208 automobiles at the park on the day that they performed.

of the Redpath-Horner Chautauqua began, with Laurant performing on the opening night.

As in Waxahachie, the Ruth Bowers Company performed on the Sunday program, which combined local personnel and the circuit talent. In the morning, there was a church service with singing by local choirs and a sermon by the dean of Bethany College. The *Cawker City Public Record* described the scene:

> Sunday morning was fair and beautiful and arrivals began with the early trains, the children and the baskets and hampers predominating. A stranger from a distance remarked that the quantity of food brought in seemed unprecedented, and the sight of groups seated on the greensward at noon time showed the quality was of the best and made a picture that should have been preserved by artists.[76]

The Ruth Bowers Company performed in both the afternoon and evening. The afternoon lecture was given by Byron Piatt and the evening program by Ralph Parlette, the editor of the *Lyceumite and Talent* magazine. After the Redpath-Horner programs, the Lincoln Park Chautauqua concluded with a weekend of local activities.

In 1911, a severe flood on the first day had resulted in a drastic drop in attendance and an incurred debt of $6,300. Attendance for the 1912

Celia Fox outside the tent where they stayed at Lincoln Park.

program was not sufficient to recoup the losses from the previous year, so that was the last chautauqua at Lincoln Park.

The Ruth Bowers Company finished the final two weeks of the 1912 season with performances in Nebraska.

The *Lyceumite and Talent* magazine reported a special event at Central City on August 19. For Eugene Laurant's thirty-seventh birthday, "Miss Ruth Bowers, Miss Pettit, Byron Piatt, Superintendents Bemmon and Shirley and his company boys interrupted him in the middle of his magic program to present him a gold watch chain."[77] Their final program was at Wayne on August 24. Laurant wrote: "We have had a great season with Horner and I am sorry to see it end. We had a farewell with Horner and our Company last night."

Horner's first year of managing his own chautauqua circuit had been very successful. Governor Joseph Folk, who had been on the 1911 Redpath-Vawter circuit, lectured for Horner during the month of July. In a letter to chautauqua manager Harry Harrison on July 20, he wrote:

Everything seems to be moving along beautifully on this circuit. The audiences I should say average one third larger than last year. If Vawter made good money last year Horner will certainly make a killing this season. Every place has been delightful and while of course some are better than others the average is very high.

HAZARDOUS PERFORMANCES IN KANSAS

The Ruth Bowers Company played at Concordia on August 3. Two nights later, a severe storm hit the area. The *Concordia Daily Blade* described its effect on the chautauqua program.

STORM SWEEPS CONCORDIA

The severest storm which Concordia has experienced in years struck the city about 8:30 last night with terrific violence, unroofing buildings, crashing in plate glass windows and tearing off limbs ...

When the storm cloud first appeared in the northwest, there were about a thousand people in the Chautauqua tent at the city park and many of them, fortunately, left before the storm struck. When the lowering cloud, twisting and swirling, suddenly seemed to drop to earth and with a fiendish attack swept over the town driving blinding sand and dust before it, there were about three hundred people in the tent and the wind snapped the guy ropes on the north side and swept the musicians and piano clear from the platform as if they were paper manikins. The tent pole outer guy ropes held and this let the tent down slowly and probably saved a good many lives. The canvas was ripped in many places and the big ropes finally gave way and let the whole tent down flat on the seats. By this time the people had been all gotten out and were on their way home in the drenching rain.

Manager Jones remained cool and when he saw the tent was going, shouted for everybody to get under the seats and this order was obeyed. The majority of the people kept their wits about them and no panic ensued. It was a lucky escape ...

When the storm struck the Chautauqua tent the Venetian Troubadours were on the stage and they were swept off by the wind, which carried the tent down into the audience. They immediately became panic stricken and began shrieking in their native tongue for one another and for assistance. Two of them ran from the park and were finally located in the west part of town, where they had taken refuge in a ditch. The rest of the troupe were gathered up by Manager Jones and piloted to their hotel, where they continued to shout and gesticulate frantically for several hours. Several of them knew but little English and one expressed his feeling by repeating, "Damn Concordia, Damma Kansa" ...

One man was heard to remark this morning that he wouldn't have minded the storm at Chautauqua grounds if the ladies had kept their hair pins and store hair out of the air. He declares that he was so busy dodging these that he forgot to see that his wife was out from the fallen tent.[78]

The newspaper noted that several people were slightly injured at the chautauqua tent, including the manager, Jones, who got a cut over his right eye when he was struck on the head by the piano as it was blown off the platform.

The same powerful storm struck the town of Belleville. The *Lyceumite and Talent* magazine included an article about it in their edition from September 1912. It described the storm at Concordia, included a photograph of the damage and provided an eyewitness account of the storm at Belleville:

> I saw one end of the big tent churn up and down in the air, slit and torn, like a collapsing balloon. The guy ropes pulled the stakes from the ground and whipped them thru the air, the two by four poles whirled, the big center pole snapped in the middle, the piano went over, smashing Mr. Chapman's silver baritone horn. The big gasoline stage light went over and a great flame shot down the stem. Some man, who is a real hero, leaped to it, turned off the gasoline and saved an explosion...Five minutes and the wind was spent, the riddled canvas fell over the wrecked seats, and a deluge of rain fell.[79]

The *Belleville Republic County* newspaper reported on the storm and its aftermath:

CHAUTAUQUA TENT WAS BLOWN DOWN AND MANY PEOPLE INJURED

Pouring rain and a violent wind caused a panic at the opening evening entertainment of the Chautauqua on Monday night. The big tent collapsed and several people were injured by falling poles.

The rain and wind commenced about 8:30 and many started to leave but were told to keep their seats as there was absolutely no danger. In a very few minutes the wind was blowing a gale. The tent was lifted clear off the ground, the loose quarter poles falling in all directions. A falling pole struck the generator of the lighting system and the darkness added to the confusion.

Women and children ran screaming in all directions. Several people were injured slightly ...

Although the tents were wrecked by the wind, Mr. Teagarden had the top patched up for the Tuesday afternoon number. All lovers of really good music were surely highly entertained by the Ruth Bowers Company both afternoon and evening. Miss Bowers is one of the greatest if not the greatest violinist of the Chautauqua platform. The lecture

"American Morals" was both interesting and instructive. Byron C. Piatt talks straight from the shoulder and says what he thinks. Laurant the illusionist pleased not only the children but their parents as well with a wonderful display of the mystic arts.[80]

On the same evening that the storm occurred, the Ruth Bowers Company performed at Smith Center about eighty kilometres (fifty miles) to the west of these two towns, and they were not affected by the weather.

Ruth and Celia from the 1912 Redpath-Horner Chautauqua program.

Celia and Ruth returning to the chautauqua tent after an automobile ride.

The season had also been successful for Ruth. She managed her own company, which consistently received favorable reviews in the press. Most days the company shared billing with one of the stars of the Redpath-Horner circuit. Ruth had a camaraderie with Celia and Gladys and with Laurant and his assistants, along with an excellent rapport with the audience.

But the 1912 chautauqua circuit occurred at a difficult time in Ruth's personal life. After five years of courtship, she and Gibby had put their relationship on hold. Indecision occupied her thoughts and made the tour less enjoyable. When Ruth and Gibby exchanged a letter in mid-August, he said: "To think I should not write you for so long and you not write me after five years of continued close relationsip." He also said: "Your mind is surely in a whirl at the time of the writing. You have my sympathy for I know and realize how miserable you are. I have been in the same condition since I left you at Erie that day."

. Despite the difficulties in her personal life, and inconveniences like the heat and lost luggage, Ruth continued to give excellent performances, please audiences and develop friendships.

PIANISSIMO

After the 1912 tour, Ruth and Gibby reconciled their differences and resumed their relationship. When they got married in 1913, she received a congratulatory telegram from Laurant and presents from several chautauqua friends. Ruth and Gibby made their residence in Pittsburgh.

The number of chautauqua circuits and performers continued to increase until 1924, which is considered the peak year of the movement. Its decline in the following years is attributed to several factors, including the automobile, which facilitated travel to larger towns; radio and motion pictures, which provided easier access to cultural events; and changing cultural tastes in American society. The Great Depression brought the final demise of circuit chautauquas in 1932. By that time, millions of Canadians and Americans had attended at least one chautauqua or lyceum program, and it had an important influence on the lives of many people (both those who performed and those who listened).

Some of the people that Ruth knew continued performing on the chautauqua and lyceum circuits. C. Edward Clarke toured for many years throughout the United States and Canada. He married Rachel Steinman, a young violinist from Des Moines he had met on a chautauqua tour, and they performed together almost until the end of the circuits. Clarke then spent some time in the music industry in Hollywood, taught singing and became a university professor in music.

Grace Desmond spent the fall of 1912 on a lyceum tour of the western United States with the famous reader and performer Katherine Ridgeway and toured with the Riner Sisters in 1913.

Elma Smith made a career of performing on the chautauqua and lyceum circuits and is considered to have been one of the most talented performers among the impersonators.

Amazingly, Fransasco Ramos convinced the Redpath Lyceum Bureau to give him one more opportunity to conduct a tour with a Spanish orchestra. Ramos still had difficult relationships with people, and he was replaced in the middle of the tour. But the concept of a Spanish orchestra was popular, and the chautauqua and lyceum circuits had a Spanish or Mexican orchestra on their tours for many years. Beginning in 1913, there was also a Spanish Ladies Orchestra that traveled throughout the United States until the late 1920s.

Gladys Pettit played on chautauqua and lyceum tours until she married John Bumstead, a chautauqua supervisor, in 1914. After her marriage, Gladys continued to have a career in music.

Celia Fox joined the Old Home Singers music group and later became a member of Laurant's company in 1915 and 1916. In 1917, she married Charles MacBride, who was also in Laurant's company. Laurant was the best man at the wedding. Laurant performed on chautauqua tours until the mid-1920s and remained a professional magician until his death in 1944.

Ruth espoused Maud Powell's exhortation to make violin playing a lifework. Although she was married and had four children, Ruth continued to perform, mainly in Pittsburgh. In 1917, Gibby (who had been in the National Guard for many years and served in the Mexican Border Conflict) enlisted in World War I. While he was stationed at Camp Hancock, Georgia, before going overseas, Ruth and her first child spent time there and she played for the soldiers. In 1918, Ruth was one of the performers at a benefit concert in Pittsburgh to assist children whose parents had died in the Armenian genocide. The same year she was one of three women who formed the Artists Ensemble Trio for the "pure love of ensemble playing." In September, the trio gave a performance at the National American Music Festival in Lockport, New York, and Ruth also had a solo program.

In 1920, KDKA in Pittsburgh became the first commercial radio station. Ruth was KDKA's first live instrumental performer, initially playing in a rudimentary tent studio. During the 1920s, she had a regular weekly program, initially with KDKA and then WCAE. Her program was carried by other radio stations and listened to by people with crystal radios, so Ruth's violin music was heard by a wide American audience.

Ruth formed her own small musical company in 1922 and it played in the Pittsburgh area for many years. In addition, she taught violin at a couple of schools and had a studio for public lessons, and she influenced many young musicians. For several years, she was on the board of directors of the city's Tuesday Musical Club, the main musical organization for women in the city. Ruth continued to play the violin until late in life.

Ruth died in 1982 at the age of ninety-four. One evening, when she was in her nineties, our family took out her photograph album. Initially she had difficulty recognizing the people in the pictures, but gradually her memories returned and for two hours she talked about what it had been like to be on tour seventy years earlier. As she closed her photo album for the final time, she looked up with a smile and said, "So much for the memories."

FOLLOWING PAGES: Ruth (seated middle) with a group of chautauqua people in 1911. To the left of Ruth, wearing the tie, is J.R. Ellison, one of the founders of the chautauqua circuit in Canada.

SOURCES CONSULTED

Books and Papers

Canning, Charlotte. *The Most American Thing in America: Circuit Chautauqua as Performance.* Iowa City: University of Iowa Press, 2007.

Harrison, Harry P. *Culture Under Canvas.* New York: Hastings, 1958.

Horner, Charles F. *Strike the Tents: The Story of Chautauqua.* Philadelphia: Dorrance & Company, 1954.

Lush, Paige Clark. "Music and Identity in Circuit Chautauqua: 1904–1932." PhD diss. paper 714, University of Kentucky, 2009.

Miller, Darrel. *Lincoln Park Chautauqua: Every Man's University.* Downs, Kansas: Miller Publishing, 2007.

Schultz, James R. *The Romance of Small-Town Chautauquas.* Columbia: University of Missouri Press, 2002.

Stott, Kelly McMichael. *Waxahachie: Where Cotton Reigned King.* Charleston, South Carolina: Arcadia Publishing, 2002.

Tapia, John E. *Circuit Chautauqua: From Rural Education to Popular Entertainment in Early Twentieth Century America.* Jefferson, North Carolina: McFarland & Company, 1997.

Wurster, Austie. "Women in Chautauqua." Unpublished seminar paper, University of Iowa, 1951.

Archival Material

Abraham Lincoln Presidential Library newspaper collection, Springfield, Illinois

Alfred Moredock Collection, Special Collections, University of Iowa, Iowa City, Iowa

Chautauqua Collection, Allegheny College, Lawrence Pelletier Library, Special Collections, Meadville, Pennsylvania

Redpath Chautauqua Collection, Special Collections, University of Iowa, Iowa City, Iowa

State Historical Society of Iowa, newspaper collection, Iowa City, Iowa

State Historical Society of Kansas, newspaper collection, Topeka, Kansas

Newspaper Citations

1   *Forest City Summit*, July 27, 1911
2   *Wellington Daily News*, July 14, 1912
3   *News Journal* (Newcastle), October 1, 1909
4   *Le Mars Semi-Weekly Sentinel*, July 18, 1911
5   *Franklin County Recorder* (Hampton), July 26, 1911
6   Erie newspaper, Ruth Bowers scrapbook
7   *Chicago Music News*, January 14, 1910
8   *Chicago Music News*, January 14, 1910
9   *Montevideo Leader*, January 21, 1910
10 *Union County Courier* (Elk Point), January 27, 1910
11 *Kingsley Times*, January 27, 1910
12 *Correctionville News*, January 27, 1910
13 *Pomeroy Herald*, January 27, 1910
14 *Hancock County Democrat* (Garner), February 3, 1910
15 *Maquoketa Excelsior*, February 8, 1910
16 *Belle Plaine Democratic Herald*, February 11, 1910
17 *Burlington Hawk Eye*, February 19, 1910
18 *Gate City Daily* (Keokuk), February 22, 1910
19 *Queen City Mail* (Spearfish), March 16, 1910
20 *News Journal* (Newcastle), March 18, 1910
21 *Ord Weekly Journal*, March 31, 1910
22 *Nebraska Telegram* (Columbus), April 1, 1910
23 Ruth Bowers scrapbook, April 3, 1910
24 *Eldorado Republican*, May 19, 1910
25 *Alton Daily Telegraph*, June 16, 1910
26 *Taylorville Daily Breeze*, June 13 to 18, 1910
27 *Illinois State Register* (Springfield), June 21, 1910
28 *Naperville Clarion*, July 27, 1910
29 *Galena Daily Gazette*, August 17, 1910
30 *Winfield Daily Free Press*, November 16, 1910
31 *Winfield Daily Chronicle*, November 16, 1910
32 *Bartlesville Morning Examiner*, November 18, 1910
33 *McIntosh County Democrat* (Checotah), November 24, 1910
34 *Lawton Daily Star*, November 27, 1910
35 *Gainesville Hesperian Daily*, December 3, 1910
36 *Hollis Post Herald*, December 22, 1910
37 *Pasco Express*, March 2, 1911
38 *Bridgeton Evening News*, February 2, 1911
39 *Punxsutawney Spirit*, February 6, 1911
40 *Lincoln County Times* (Davenport), March 10, 1911
41 *Nanaimo Free Press*, March 10, 1911
42 *Marysville Globe*, October 14, 1910

43   *Marysville Globe*, March 18, 1911
44   *Klamath Falls Daily*, March 23, 1911
45   *Franklin County Recorder* (Hampton), July 26, 1911
46   *West Liberty Index*, June 29, 1911
47   *Cedar Rapids Republican*, June 30, 1911
48   *Le Mars Semi-Weekly Sentinel*, July 11 and 18, 1911
49   *Forest City Summit*, July 20, 1911
50   *Woodbine Twiner*, July 27, 1911
51   *Denison Bulletin*, July 26, 1911
52   *Mt. Pleasant Daily Journal*, August 3, 1911
53   *Adams County Press* (Corning), July 19, 1911
54   *Estherville Vindicator and Republican*, June 21, 1911
55   *Warrenton Banner*, September 1, 1911
56   *Lyceumite and Talent*, Volume 6, July 1912, p.35
57   *Cheyenne State Leader*, June 20, 1912
58   Lamar, Ruth Bowers scrapbook
59   *Dodge City Globe*, June 28, 1912
60   *Newton Journal*, July 4, 1912
61   *Woodson County Advocate*, July 1, 1912
62   *Yates Center News*, July 5, 1912
63   *Wilson County Citizen* (Fredonia), July 5, 1912
64   *Denton Record and Chronicle*, July 6, 1912
65   *Gainesville Daily Register*, July 9, 1912
66   *Hennessey Clipper*, July 9, 1912
67   *Waxahachie Light*, July 9, 1912
68   *Enid Daily Eagle*, July 11 and 12, 1912
69   *Arkansas City Daily Traveler*, July 10, 1912
70   *Wellington Daily News*, July 13 and 16, 1912
71   *Kingman Leader Courier*, July 25, 1912
72   *Kinsley Mercury*, July 25, 1912
73   *Marion Record*, July 25, 1912
74   *Wamego Reporter*, August 1, 1912
75   *Hays Free Press*, August 3, 1912
76   *Cawker City Public Record*, August 8, 1912
77   *Lyceumite and Talent*, Volume 6, September 1912, p. 51.
78   *Concordia Daily Blade*, August 6, 1912
79   *Lyceumite and Talent*, Volume 6, September 1912, p.63.
80   *Belleville Republic County Democrat*, August 7, 1912

APPENDIX

Ruth Bowers Tour Itineraries

This is a list of the dates and places where Ruth played on her chautauqua and lyceum tours. It is based on her notes, newspaper articles, and chautauqua and lyceum itineraries. The itinerary is virtually complete for the 1910 and 1911 chautauqua tours and the lyceum tour with the Ramos Spanish Orchestra. The Nebraska part of the 1912 Chautauqua circuit is particularly incomplete. When Ruth performed in a different state from the preceding entry the name of the state is listed.

January – March 1910
Lyceum tour – Ramos'
Spanish Orchestra

Jan. 8 Northwood, IA
Jan. 11 – Warren, MN
Jan. 12 – Crookston
Jan. 13 – Sandstone
Jan. 14 – Hutchinson
Jan. 15 – Montevideo
Jan. 17 – Rock Rapids, IA
Jan. 18 – Scotland, SD
Jan. 19 – Springfield
Jan. 21 – Elk Point
Jan. 22 – Kingsley, IA
Jan. 24 – Correctionville
Jan. 25 – Marcus
Jan. 26 – Pomeroy
Jan 27 – Goldfield
Jan. 28 – Garner
Jan. 29 – Canton, MN (missed performance)
Jan. 30 – McGregor, IA
Jan. 31 – Waukon
Feb. 1 – Riceville
Feb. 2 – Austin, MN
Feb. 3 – Plainview
Feb. 4 – Hopkinton, IA
Feb. 5 – Walcott
Feb. 7 – Maquoketa
Feb. 8 – Tipton
Feb. 9 – Belle Plaine
Feb. 10 – Zearing
Feb. 11 – Winterset
Feb. 12 – Afton

Feb. 14 – Keota
Feb. 15 – Knoxville
Feb. 16 – Monroe
Feb. 17 – Brighton
Feb. 18 – Burlington
Feb. 19 – Olds
Feb. 21 – Keokuk
Feb. 22 – Centerville
Feb. 23 – Mt. Ayr
Feb. 24 – Lamoni
Feb. 25 – Villisca
Feb. 26 – Dexter
Feb. 28 – Blair, NE
Mar. 1 – Albion
Mar. 2 – West Point
Mar. 3 – Stanton
Mar. 4 – Norfolk
Mar. 5 – Ponca
Mar. 7 – O'Neill
Mar. 8 – Valentine
Mar. 9 – Gordon
Mar. 10 – Crawford
Mar. 11 – Spearfish, SD
Mar. 12 – Belle Fourche
Mar. 14 – Lead
Mar. 15 – Edgemont
Mar. 16 – Newcastle, WY
Mar. 17 – Alliance, NE
Mar. 18 – Lexington
Mar. 19 – North Platte
Mar. 21 – Broken Bow
Mar. 22 - Kearney
Mar. 23 – Sidney
Mar. 24 – Ord

Mar. 25 – Silver Creek
Mar. 26 - Gibbon
Mar. 27 – Columbus

May – October 1910 –
Chautauqua tour –
Elma B. Smith Company

All locations are in Illinois
May 17 – Mound City
May 18 – Eldorado
May 19 – Shawneetown
May 20 – Marion
May 21, 22 – Metropolis
May 24 – Pinckneyville
May 25 – Coulterville
May 26 – Nashville
May 27 – Anna
May 28, 29 – Benton
May 31 – West Salem
June 1 – Albion
June 2 – Flora
June 3 – Mount Carmel
June 4, 5 – Robinson
June 7 – Newton
June 8 – Toledo
June 9 – Marshall
June 10 – Kinmundy
June 11, 12 – Olney
June 14 – Girard
June 15 – Alton
June 16 – Taylorville
June 17 – Mt. Auburn
June 18, 19 – Auburn
June 21 – Sullivan

June 23 – Potomac
June 24 – Hoopeston
June 25, 26 – Tuscola
June 28 – Talulla
June 29 – Mason City
une 30 – Atlanta
July 1 – Pekin
July 2,3 – Delavan
July 5 – Saybrook
July 7 – Stanford
July 8 – LeRoy
July 9,10 – Farmer City
July 12 – Sheldon
July 13 – Fairbury
July 14 – El Paso
July 15 – Gibson City
July 16, 17 – Onarga
July 19 – Sparland
July 20 – Morris
July 21 – Leland
July 22 – Wenona
July 23, 24 – Washburn
July 26 – Naperville
July 27 – Newark
July 28 – Plainfield
July 29 – Waterman
July 30, 31 – La Moille
Aug. 2 – Austin
Aug. 3 – Wheaton
Aug. 4 – Harvey
Aug. 5 – Peotone
Aug. 6, 7 – Downers Grove
Aug. 9 – Pecatonica
Aug. 10 – Elgin
Aug. 11 – Barrington
Aug. 12 – Harvard
Aug. 13, 14 – Belvidere
Aug. 16 – Galena
Aug. 17 – Mt. Carroll
Aug. 18 – Warren
Aug. 19 – Stockton
Aug. 20, 21 – Polo
Aug. 23 – Erie
Aug. 24 – Franklin Grove
Aug. 25 – Oregon
Aug. 26 – Morrison
Aug. 27, 28 – Port Byron
Aug. 30 – Viola
Aug. 31 – Toulon

Sep. 1 – Streator
Sep. 2 – Oneida
Sep. 3,4 – Woodhull
Sep. 6 – Roseville
Sep. 7 – Stronghurst
Sep. 8 – Abingdon
Sep. 9 – London Mills
Sep. 10, 11 – Lewiston
Sep. 13 – Industry
Sep. 14 – Carthage
Sep. 15 – Plymouth
Sep. 16 – Colchester
Sep. 17, 18 – Rushville
Sep. 20 – Kinderhook
Sep. 21 – Carrollton
Sep. 22 – Winchester
Sep. 23 – Mt. Sterling
Sep. 24, 25 – Clayton
Sep. 27 – Carlyle
Sep. 28 – Lebanon
Sep. 29 – Litchfield
Sep. 30 – New Douglas
Oct. 1,2 – Greenville

**November – December 1910 –
Lyceum tour – Elma B. Smith
Company**

Nov. 14 – Cherokee, KS
Nov. 15 – Winfield
Nov. 16 – Kaw City, OK
Nov. 17 – Bartlesville
Nov. 18 – Collinsville
Nov. 19 – Afton
Nov. 21 – Tulsa
Nov. 22 – Checotah
Nov. 23 - Quinton
Nov. 25 – Stroud
Nov. 26 – Lawton
Nov. 28 – Snyder
Nov. 30 - Waurika
Dec. 2 – Gainesville, TX
Dec. 3 - Bowie
Dec. 5 - Nocona
Dec. 10 – Canyon
Dec. 12 – Canadian
Dec. 13 – McLean
Dec. 14 - Shamrock
Dec. 15 – Clinton, OK
Dec. 17 – Lone Wolf

Dec. 19 – Hollis
Dec. 20 – El Dorado
Dec. 21 – Granite
Dec. 22 - Arapaho

**January – March 1911 –
Lyceum tour – Elma B. Smith
Company**

Jan. 16 – Kane, PA
Jan. 17 – Emporium
Jan. 19 – Greene
Jan. 21 – Leesport
Jan. 24 – Wycombe
Jan. 25 – Chatham
Jan. 26 – Bridgeville, DE
Jan. 27 – Georgetown
Jan. 30 – Camden, NJ
Jan. 31 – Elmer
Feb. 1 – Bridgeton
Feb. 2 – Trenton
Feb. 3 – Brogueville, PA
Feb. 4 – Punxsutawney
Feb. 6 - Millersburg
Feb. 7 – Gettysburg
Feb. 15 – Chicago, IL
Feb. 17 – Augusta
Feb. 18 – Golden
Feb. 20 – Quincy
Feb. 21 – Litchfield
Feb. 24 – Vermillion, SD
Feb. 25 – Yankton
Mar. 2 – Wilber, WA
Mar. 3 – Davenport
Mar. 4 – Odessa
Mar. 6 – Pasco
Mar. 7 – Prosser
Mar. 8 – Mabton
Mar. 9 – Outlook
Mar. 10 – Granger
Mar. 13 – Nanaimo, BC
Mar. 14 – Vancouver
Mar. 15 – Burlington, WA
Mar. 16 – Marysville
Mar. 17 – Skykomish
Mar. 18 – Castle Rock
Mar. 20 – Cottage Grove, OR
Mar. 21 - Ashland
Mar. 22 – Klamath Falls
June – September 1911

– Chautauqua tour–
Clarke-Bowers Company

June 28 – West Liberty, IA
June 29 – Cedar Rapids
June 30 – Belle Plaine
July 1 – Grundy Center
July 2 – Traer
July 3 – Independence
July 4 – Manchester
July 5 – Waverly
July 6 – Osage
July 7 – New Hampton
July 8 – Waukon
July 10 – Austin, MN
July 11 – Mankato
July 12 – Marshall
July 13 – LeMars, IA
July 14 – Cherokee
July 15 – Sheldon
July 16 – Luverne, MN
July 17 – Sibley, IA
July 18 – Estherville
July 19 – Forest City
July 20 – Northwood
July 21 – Hampton
July 22 – Eldora
July 24 – Woodbine
July 25 – Denison
July 26 – Audubon
July 27 – Perry
July 28 – Stuart
July 29 – Newton
July 30 – Montezuma
July 31 – Hedrick
Aug. 1 – Ottumwa
Aug. 2 – Mt. Pleasant
Aug. 3 – Greenfield
Aug. 4 – Corning
Aug. 5 – Osceola
Aug. 6 – Leon
Aug. 7 – Mt. Ayr
Aug. 8 – Grant City, MO
Aug. 9 – Albany
Aug. 10 – Stanberry
Aug. 11 – Savannah
Aug. 12 – Princeton
Aug. 13 – Seymour, IA
Aug. 14 – Memphis, MO
Aug. 15 – Lancaster

Aug. 16 – Milan
Aug. 17 – Edina
Aug. 18 – Macon
Aug. 19 – Shelbina
Aug. 20 – Palmyra
Aug. 21 – Canton
Aug. 22 – Louisiana
Aug. 23 – Montgomery
Aug. 24 – Warrenton
Aug. 25 – Fulton
Aug. 26 – Centralia
Aug. 27 – Fayette
Aug. 28 – Salisbury
Aug. 29 – Carrolton
Aug. 30 – Richmond
Aug. 31 – Holden
Sep. 1 – Odessa
Sep. 2 – Marshall
Sep. 3 – Mexico

June – August 1912 –
Chautauqua tour –
Ruth Bowers Company

June 17 – Sterling, CO
June 19 – Cheyenne, WY
June 20 – Fort Collins, CO
June 22 – Canon City
June 24 – Lamar
June 27 – Dodge City, KS
June 28 – Newton
June 29 – Yates Center
July 1 – Fredonia
July 2 – Pawnee, OK
July 3 – Stillwater
July 4 – Guthrie
July 5 – Denton, TX
July 7 – Waxahachie
July 9 – Gainesville
July 11 – Enid, OK
July 12 – Arkansas City, KS
July 13 – Ponca City, OK
July 14 – Wellington, KS
July 16 – Kingman
July 17 – Pratt
July 18 – Stafford
July 19 – Kinsley
July 20 – Larned
July 21 – Great Bend
July 22 - McPherson

July 23 – Marion
July 24 – El Dorado
July 26 – Garnett
July 27 - Paola
July 28 – Wamego
July 29 – Junction City
July 30 – Hays
July 31 – Russell
Aug. 1 – Ellsworth
Aug. 2 – Abilene
Aug. 3 – Concordia
Aug. 4 – Lincoln Park
Aug. 5 – Smith Center
Aug. 6 – Belleville
Aug. 8 – Blue Rapids
Aug. 12 – McCook, NE
Aug. 19 – Central City
Aug. 22 – Wahoo
Aug. 25 – Wayne
Other known venues in Nebraska – Fairfield, Aurora

INDEX

P

Pasco (WA) 120, 121, 217
Pawnee (OK) 191, 193
Pawnee Bill's Ranch 192, 193
Peck, Arthur 138, 139, 140, 145, 146, 148, 155, 162, 163, 164, 171, 174
Pettit, Gladys 200, 203, 204, 207, 213
Philadelphia (PA) 114, 116
Piano and pianist 11, 33, 37, 42, 45, 47, 54, 60, 76, 77, 78, 81, 91, 94, 100, 104, 105, 106, 114, 125, 133, 139, 145, 147, 148, 151, 156, 157, 164, 172, 181, 184, 187, 200, 208, 209
Piatt, Byron 182, 183, 189, 190, 196, 204, 206, 207, 210
Picnic 105, 204, 206
Pikes Peak 183, 184
Pittsburgh (PA) 13, 33, 34, 39, 156, 212
Plainfield (IL) 91, 92, 93
Pomeroy (IA) 52, 217
Powell, Maud 181, 184, 191, 213
Pratt Institute 33, 34
Prince George Hotel 116
Punxsutawney (PA) 118, 217

R

Ramos, Franasco 36, 37, 38, 40, 42
Ramos Spanish Orchestra 34, 37, 38, 39, 40, 41, 42, 44
Reader 25, 120, 133, 212
Redpath, James 19, 20
Regina, Antonio 37, 42, 44, 48, 51, 53, 58, 59, 60, 63, 64, 67, 68, 69, 73
Ridgeway, Katherine 133, 212
Riner Sisters 133, 141, 212
Ringgold (TX) 106
Robley, Bayard 179
Robley Quartet 126, 127
Rock Rapids (IA) 42, 43, 155
Rockford (IL) 91
Rohde, Julius 40, 42, 43, 46, 47, 48, 49, 51, 53, 54, 55, 57, 58, 62, 64, 135, 148, 153, 156, 161, 162, 174

S

Sandstone (MN) 40
Saxophone 181, 183, 184, 187, 196
Schradieck, Henry 180, 181
Schubert 34, 145, 201
Seasholes, Dr. Charles 82, 87, 140, 147
Seattle (WA) 121
Serenade (Schubert) 145, 201
Seymour (MO) 170, 172
Sibley (IA) 156
Skykomish (WA) 126
Smith, Elma B. 74, 75, 76, 77, 78, 80, 81, 83, 86, 88, 91, 94, 98, 100, 103, 104, 105, 106, 112, 113, 127
Smith, Nettie 120, 126, 127
Spanish Orchestra 64, 69, 70, 71, 72
Spearfish (SD) 67, 68, 217
Spokane (WA) 121
Springfield (IL) 85, 87, 90
Sterling (CO) 182, 183
Storm 27, 43, 62, 82, 156, 208-210
Sun dance 102, 192, 193

T

Taylorville (IL) 81, 82, 84, 85, 217
Thaviu, A.F. 135
Thaviu's International Band 11, 30, 133, 140
Traer (IA) 148
Train 24, 27, 30, 31, 43, 44, 54, 55, 60, 65, 66, 75, 99, 103, 110, 143, 155, 156, 158, 159, 162, 163, 170, 182, 183, 206
Traumerei 45, 78, 79, 87, 156, 201
Trumpet 134, 136, 138
Trunk 30, 31, 40, 49, 57, 183, 201, 205
Tulsa (OK) 104

V

Vancouver (BC) 119, 121, 122-124
Vawter, Keith 20, 21, 56, 129, 133, 147, 149, 166, 179
Venetian Troubadours 208
Vermillion (SD) 118, 119
Violin 11, 13, 14, 17, 18, 30, 32, 33, 34, 35, 42, 43, 44, 45, 54, 60, 63, 67, 69, 70, 72, 75, 78, 91, 94, 100, 104, 105, 106, 110, 114, 115, 117, 142, 145, 147, 157, 164, 174, 180, 181, 182, 184, 190, 191, 198, 200, 201, 203, 204, 213

W

Waldorf Astoria 180
Walcott (IA) 56, 57
Ward, J.H. 204
Warrenton (MO) 173, 174, 218
Waukon (IA) 151, 152, 153
Waverly (IA) 150
Waxahachie (TX) 194-196
Weatherwax Brothers Quartet 11, 133, 134, 135, 136, 138, 166
Wellington (KS) 26, 199, 200, 217, 218
West Liberty (IA) 142, 218
West Texas Normal School 108, 110
White Rose Orchestra 137, 140
Wilson, Alonzo 21, 77, 78, 86
Wilson, Elma B. 120
Winfield (KS) 99, 100, 217
Winona (IN) 174, 179
Winter, Clara 191
Woodbine (IA) 158, 159, 162, 163, 218

Y

Yankton (SD) 44, 120
Yates Center (KS) 188-191, 218

Z

Zigeunerweisen 34, 100, 101, 104, 117, 132, 156